Psychic Abilities

*Unlocking Aura Reading, Clairvoyance,
and Telepathy*

Your Free Gift (only available for a limited time)

Thanks for getting this book! If you want to learn more about various spirituality topics, then join Mari Silva's community and get a free guided meditation MP3 for awakening your third eye. This guided meditation mp3 is designed to open and strengthen ones third eye so you can experience a higher state of consciousness. Simply visit the link below the image to get started.

https://spiritualityspot.com/meditation

Table of Contents

Part 1: Auras

The Ultimate Guide to Aura Reading, Clairvoyance, and Other Psychic Abilities

Introduction

Have you ever experienced someone tell you how you must be feeling, or what mood you were in just by looking at you? Did you ask how they knew this without you giving them a hint? Several people, including myself, have come across people with this "magic power." They can tell when someone is feeling sad, happy, anxious, and even, downright depressed. At the time, I wondered how they did it. I had to know – so I just asked. Their response was simple, "I can see everything." They didn't have an explanation as to why or how they could do this, but they just found they could see what mood someone was in simply by seeing colors around their head and body. Neither of us knew what they were seeing was someone's aura. I honestly didn't even fully comprehend what an aura was! This is called aura awareness. You will see things at the ordinary person cannot detect and so much more.

People are sometimes scared to seek knowledge about specific subjects and issues. Often, this is usually due to the sentiments attached to the subject. One topic that people run from is reading auras. You have likely heard people talk about auras before, or you may have come across things on the internet that piqued your interests. It doesn't matter where you first learned about auras. If you are reading this, you have successfully overwritten your fear of rightfully seeking knowledge about auras.

It is commonly believed that only people who deal with spirituality can do things such as seeing and reading auras, but this is not true. Although a person will require a certain spiritual awareness before they can start, anybody can learn to see and read auras. Now, you are probably wondering how you can do that. Not to worry, this is precisely why this book has been written to serve as a guide to auras and aura reading. This book serves as your ultimate guide to reading auras and developing other psychic abilities such as clairvoyance. You will require no additional resources to learn everything there is to know about auras and the auric field.

In this book, you will be privy to a wealth of information about the esoteric beliefs and practices surrounding auras. The first chapter has information about the aura itself and the auric field. It covers all the basics about the energy field from the shape and size of the aura, to the aura's purpose. There is also a subchapter dedicated to answering the most asked questions about the aura. From there, the rest of the book focuses on explaining and providing detailed information on aura anatomy, reading, protection, and cleansing. You will learn about the colors of the aura and what they stand for.

When you see a person's aura, the color will give you insight into the feelings and thoughts of that person. You will also learn how you can develop the ability to heal your own aura, and those of others. Finally, you will find daily tips to help you nurture and develop your psychic abilities so you can affect the people around you and the world. From beginning to end, you will acquire more information on auras than you'll likely find anywhere else.

Without further delay, let's get start learning about auras and other psychic abilities!

Chapter One: What is an Aura?

The question, "What is an aura?" is one relatively straightforward to answer. As you may already know, humans, including you, are spiritual beings existing in physical bodies. An energy field thus surrounds every human. This energy field is called the *aura*. Your aura is the body of energy that either shines brightly or dully, depending on the state it is in. But humans are not the only ones with auras; plants and animals do too. Every living thing has its own aura. Although you may not see it, your pet has a body of energy surrounding it, and so do the plants in your gardens.

The aura is generally defined as an energy field that encloses all people, animals, and things. Many people erroneously believe that it is only discussed in spiritual circles. Still science recognizes the existence of auras. Scientists have found evidence to believe that everything from nature emits an electromagnetic energy. Its concept isn't an unreasonable or ludicrous thing made up by certain people, as most believe. Without a doubt, you have met people and gotten a certain feeling or vibe from them. For instance, one individual might make you feel nervous and anxious, while another makes you feel relaxed. Well, this has everything to do with their aura. The aura informs a person's general attitude and disposition, and individuals can usually feel it. Learning about auras can give you more insight into your relationships with yourself, those around you, as well as nature. Your aura is of great emotional and spiritual significance, as you will realize the further you go in this book.

Your physical body operates through the flow of life that comes from your energy field. The energy field, also called the auric field, consists of seven layers connected to your physical body. The seven auric layers are the link between your spiritual body and your physical body. The general belief is that all a person's emotions, experiences, and memories are in the auric field, therefore, it's one place where psychics can get information about a person. The field is also connected to the chakra system. It is a non-physical entity, and that is why you cannot see it with the naked eyes unless you put in some practice.

Many people who can see or sense it say it is in the shape of an egg. Others describe it as a cocoon-shaped entity. Some say that the aura roughly follows the contours of the physical body. When you see the aura, it may be close to someone's physical body. For others, it may be immensely expanded from the body. Many things can affect the size of the aura and its proximity to the body. You might pull the aura closer to you when you feel tense, frightened, or uncertain. Here, it will be just a few inches from your body. It pulls in to help you feel protected in intense situations. This is why some people feel something enclosing and wrapping around them when scared or tense.

But if you feel relaxed, confident, and safe, the aura expands several inches away from the body. Sometimes it may expand beyond. Your aura can extend to somewhere as distant as infinity. The position in proximity to the body depends on the situation an individual is in, but the consensus is that the aura is typically six inches away from the body. When closer to the body, the aura naturally becomes denser. As its distance from the body increases, it becomes lighter, more transparent, and more refined.

Let's get into the science of the aura and auric field. According to science, the physical body comprises biological circuits that transport electric currents through the human organism's wiring systems. The transportable electric currents are generated in several layers, forming an electromagnetic field around the human body. This electromagnetic field is what we all know as an aura, and it is very much recognized in science. In fact, it can be photographed. Different research methods and techniques, such as electrophotography, confirm that all existing matter have this electromagnetic field. In inanimate matters, the auric field rarely experiences changes, and if changed, are minimal.

But living things have been proven to experience continuous changes in the auric field. Your aura, as a human, is directly connected to your health and well-being. Things such as physical and mental vitality, emotional clarity, and mental stability all make the auric field radiate brighter than ever. Poor health and well-being, conversely, results in a dim and weaker auric field. Many people overlook the significance of this simple fact. It is more than a representation or reflection of your inner state. More important, it is your first defense against potentially damaging factors, whether environmental, spiritual, or emotional. It also plays a vital role in how you make your decisions and how you communicate with people, verbally or otherwise.

An interesting thing to note about the aura is that it operates on the laws of attraction. You attract people with the relative energy of your auric field. Only people with similar internal vibrations as you have the chance of getting close to you. All humans can sense energy, no matter how subtle. It is common for a person to feel another individual's presence without physically seeing them. Sometimes, one can also become overwhelmed by negative energy from another individual. It is just like when you get a bad vibe from someone. If you have a powerful and vibrant aura, you are unlikely to be affected by the forces of negative energies surrounding you. Instead, you will come with peace and calm wherever you go. But people with weaker auras are quickly affected by hostile forces. Therefore, you must dedicate time and cultivate the self-discipline to manage your inner vibrations effectively to keep your aura healthy and vibrant.

When your auric field is healthy, the energy flows more freely. As a result, you can more positively responsive to thoughts, emotions, and events, and the energy of objects, people, and places. A healthy energy field protects and shields you while simultaneously helping you absorb what you need. The health of a person's auric field is generally affected by their thoughts and feelings. Positive thoughts, emotions, and experiences strengthen and improve the health of your auric field.

Conversely, negative thoughts disrupt the auric field. The experience of trauma can cause auric, energy-based "wounds" that are difficult to heal. You will learn more about healing as you go further in the book. Take note that energy sometimes gets "stuck" in the field. Everything that happens to the physical body starts in the auric field. When there is a disruption of energy in the field, over time, it can can cause health dysfunctions. It also contributes to illnesses and diseases. Simply put, sickness, diseases, and dysfunction begin in the energy field before manifesting in the physical body.

Before I delve deeper, below are the most asked questions about auras.

Commonly Asked Questions about the Aura and Auric Field

There are so many things to know about the aura, so much information to learn and use. To give you a more helpful insight into auras right before we go deeper, I answer some of the most asked questions by people new to auras and aura-reading.

1. How Real is the Aura?

Yes, it is authentic. Although the interpretation commonly varies in philosophy, it is general knowledge they exist. As I mentioned before, all matters emit energy. This energy is your aura, and the energy field is your auric field. The best way to think of auras as a beginner is the "vibe" you get from someone. This vibe comes from the energy that radiates, and this energy could be good or bad. This explains why one person might make you nervous, and another might make you feel relaxed. How you feel about someone is the reaction of your own auric field to the energy that a person emits.

2. Is Aura the Same as a Vibe?

Well, yes. If you didn't already know, "vibe" is short for vibrational frequency, which is basically what the auric field is made of. You can feel when someone around is happy, excited, sad, distraught, or nervous, even without them telling you anything. Likewise, people can "tell" when you are happy, sad, angry, or elated without you telling them a word. This is all because you can tap into that person's vibrational frequency, on which they are operating. Your vibe or aura is what people sense from you. It can either attract or repel them from you, depending on their compatibility with your frequency.

3. Do All Humans Have Auras?

Every human has an electromagnetic energy field operating around them. Other living objects also have their own energy fields. Some individuals believe that humans have a more complex energy field because of evolution.

4. What Do Auras Look Like?

A person's aura typically comprises multiple colors captured on camera made specifically for that purpose. The colors of the aura are likened to the colors of the rainbow. The vibrancy of the colors in your aura will depend on your inner state and vibrational frequency. The colors are usually brighter and more radiant when operating on a healthy frequency. They also become dimmer and weaker when the frequency isn't so strong. The aura, through aural photography, is said to be an egg-shaped or cocoon-shaped oval around the human body. People who have seen it describe it as a halo surrounding the body.

5. Can You Actually "See" Auras?

Absolutely, you can see your own or that of anybody else. Typically, you can see and capture your aura through unique cameras designed for aural photography, but if you put into practice, you can see it through other methods. For example, you can see the aura by softly squinting your eyes and looking in a mirror. To achieve this, you will need some form of practice involving dedication. The best way to pick it up is through your peripheral vision. What this means is focusing on the aura won't make you see it. But when you take your eyes away, you are likely to see the light and colors appear. Personally, the aura first came as a fuzz of white light. And then I saw the colors over time. You must dedicate your time and attention to practice to start seeing auras or reading them.

6. Is Seeing Other People's Auras Easy?

Not exactly. Seeing someone else's depends on several factors. When trying to see your own aura, you can easily meditate, focus, and dedicate time to communicating with your personal spiritual energy, but you have little to no control over these things in other people. For you to see another person's aura, they must be still. Now, unless someone comes to you for a reading, it can be tricky to tell them to stand still and let you see theirs. Fortunately, specific individuals have more vibrant and pronounced auras than others, so their auras are easier to see than others.

7. Why Does the Aura Have Multiple Colors?

The auric field comprises seven layers. Each layer is represented by one color which differs from the rest. Experts in aura reading believe that the range and interactions between the aura's colors reflect how complex a person is, physically, emotionally, and spiritually. For instance, some colors can be brighter, depending on how vibrant you are. Some may be dim and dull, depending on your emotional or physical state. And some people simply have no colors in their auras. This is not regarded as a call for concern. I explain aura colors and what they mean in chapter seven.

8. Can the Aura Change?

Over time, the auric field can go through changes. As you or may not already know, energy changes. All matters experience energy changes. There is no definitive or set formula for auric energy, and it is different for everyone due to some factors. Naturally, your thoughts, feelings, and experiences have a significant and real impact on the appearance of your aura. So, if you have a dim and weak aura now, that can change over time. It doesn't remain the same way forever.

9. Can the Aura be Cleansed?

Using a variety of methods and techniques, it can be cleansed, healed, and repaired. Subsequently, you will become privy to these methods and techniques. Some people also wonder whether it can be "turned off." This is impossible. As long as you cannot turn your thoughts and emotions off, you cannot turn the aura off. Your aura is a part of you. Think of it as a spiritual and energy-based organ without which your physical body cannot function.

10. What Happens if You Can't Sense Your Aura?

It takes time to start sensing the aura. Be ready to put the work and effort into it. Cleansing and healing it takes even longer to learn. Humans are fixated with the physical body. We devote our time to taking care of our physical bodies, but it can be much more helpful to focus on the aura. Suppose you devote more of your time to taking care of your aura and getting regular information on it through readings. There, you will inadvertently lessen your experience of pain and hardship. If you keep it clean and robust, you will find yourself in a much better position to live the life you desire and rightly deserve.

Many people, possibly including you, want to know if aura readings are legitimate. Well, it can be difficult to convince someone that something is real until they have experienced that thing. The best way to discover if aura reading is real is to dedicate your time to practice it. You will be amazed at how many benefits you stand to reap just by doing this. Conclusively, think of the aura as your representation of the connection between your physical and spiritual body. To understand and become spiritually aware of it, you need a lot of time and dedication. But eventually, the effort you put into practice can make a difference in your overall health and well-being.

In the next chapter, you will discover what exactly energy is and everything it entails!

Chapter Two: It All Starts with Energy

As you have already learned, every creation in existence comprises a body of electromagnetic energy that vibrates at varying frequencies in correspondence to sound, light, and color. This is known as the aura and has been scientifically proven to exist. This body of electromagnetic energy is considered the life force of every living thing. It is the energy of the universe. You can refer to this energy by many things, such as chi, prana, and vital life force. If you are a fan of Dr. Strange, the Marvel Comics superhero, you have probably watched him controlling this in the movies. Although these movies don't portray the depth of chi, they give valuable insight into energy.

The chi or energy is the vital life force that flows within you. Whether or not you can feel and use it or not, you are full of chi energy. Chi exists in every cell of your body, and your mind and soul. This flows through your body pathways, also known as chakras, to help you maintain physical, mental, emotional, and spiritual health and wellbeing. When you correctly harness your life force, you remain in a balanced and healthy state. The energy, or life force, links your body, spirit, and mind and unites them. This is how you become a complete person. To achieve this balanced state, you need an understanding of how your energy flows through your seven chakras, but before you get to that, you need a more in-depth explanation of energy and the energy field.

Humans have many energy fields. First, you have the physically determinable magnetic and electromagnetic energy fields present in the cells, tissues, and organs of all living objects and the human body. But you also have the biofields, which originate from these electromagnetic fields and other subtle energy bodies, pathways, and every other aspect of self. The morphogenetic field is one of the essential biofields in humans. In biology, a morphogenetic field comprises a body of cells that go directly to specific structures and organs in the human body.

An example is the cardiac energy field, which becomes the heart tissue. The first scientist to make the discovery about the morphogenetic fields is Rupert Sheldrake. According to Sheldrake, every morphic unit has an energy field within. This energy forms the morphic unit. All living things in the same group align with the morphic field to shape and develop. The morphogenetic field gives all living organisms their forms.

Essentially, the morphogenetic field contains data and information key to shaping the physical form of a living thing and possibly its behavior and relation with other living things.

The etheric field is another biofield, commonly called a *subtle energy body*. It is sometimes called the *aura*. Every life unit has individual etheric fields, from a cell to tissue, plant, and human. There is also a specific etheric field that connects with the body. The word "etheric" is derived from the word ether, regarded as an element that permeates space. The ether transmits waves of energy to the physical body, so the etheric field is also known as the physical body's energy system. The etheric field is a vital part of the energy field because it covers the entire body. It connects your physical body with other subtle energy bodies in the energy field. To understand energy concerning your life experiences, you need to understand the etheric field that serves as the physical body's energy system.

This field is the densest of the subtle energy fields, just after the physical body, dense. The etheric field is home to three major components of the energy field as a whole: the nadis, chakras, and the aura. Your etheric body exists to provide energy to your physical body so you can experience life. To put it in simpler terms, your etheric body is a separate energy field that directly connects your physical body with other subtle energy fields, serving as the source for physical growth and development. Your etheric field exists before your cells, tissues, organs, and body grow.

The etheric field comprises three vital components: the nadis, chakras, and aura. Anybody who has ever dabbled into yoga knows there are three significant nadis in the physical body. These are the ida, the Pingala, and the Sushumna. Apart from the three significant nadis, we have other minor nadis that all sum up about 72,000 in the body. These nadis, both major and minor, transmit and deliver little energy streams to your chakras and the aura within your physical body. In the etheric field, you also have thousands of chakras vital to your physical body's survival. There is a chakra for every organ, gland, and joint in your body. This results in a complex system where the chakras feed your physical body energy, the chakras are fed by the minor nadis, and the three primary nadis feed the minor nadis. Of the thousands of chakras that exist within the physical body, there are seven essential ones you have likely heard about. Let's delve into this.

The chakra system is a network of different energy channels, which, although complex, connects your body in ways you may not yet understand. The chakra itself is Sanskrit for "wheel." Thus, the chakra system spins wheels of energy throughout the body. You can think of the chakra system as your body's spiritual nervous system. The chakras are regarded as the body's energy centers because they play a vital role in getting energy across every physical body part, but the seven chakras are the main energy centers. More likely, you must have heard something about unblocking the chakras to let the energy flow. This is due to the chakras being energy centers supposed to be open at all times. Usually, the chakras should be open so energy can flow through them freely. The purpose of this is to create a state of harmony between the body, mind, and spirit. But sometimes, the chakras become blocked due to physical or emotional problems and stress. When this happens, it becomes difficult for the energy system to run as efficiently as it does typically, resulting in problems. The consequences of an ineffective or irregular energy flow system can range from physical discomfort to ailments or emotional imbalance.

I should briefly note that "energy" is an ambiguous word that can be interpreted differently. The ambiguity of this word makes it hard to understand just what the energy system represents. Many people talk about "energy" without knowing what they are talking about. I should also note that energy cannot be explained or understood from a couple of thousand words, but understanding the chakra system makes the energy system much easier to understand. The chakra system makes it possible to explain the movement and delivery of energy/chi/life force, and yourself. Learning to work with your chakras and learning how to keep them in a balanced state can do many things for you. The most basic of these are improving your emotional state, curing illnesses, and even opening up a path to financial success.

The chakra system consists of seven chakras that exist alongside your spine. The chakras begin at your perineum, between your anus and genitals, and runs directly to the apex of your head. The top chakra can be found above the top of your head, just outside the body. Each chakra vibrates at a different frequency from the others and is represented by a different color peculiar to it. Knowing and memorizing the colors of the chakras is vital for chakra visualization meditation. Note that each chakra is also associated with particular organs, emotions, and functions. Without taking more time, below are the seven chakras from bottom to top and what they represent.

The first chakra is the Root Chakra, which is also called *Muladhara*. This chakra represents the human foundation. Within the physical body, the root chakra is at the base of your spine, the reason it is called the "root" chakra. It provides that feeling of being grounded. When energy flows through the root chakra, it gives you the confidence to stand up to challenges and overcome obstacles, but when this chakra is blocked and energy cannot flow through, it produces a feeling of instability and threat, making it difficult to stand on one's two feet against challenges and obstacles. The root chakra is tied with your survival as a human. Its primary color is red.

The Sacral Chakra is the second chakra. You may also call it the *Swadisthana*. This chakra is located a couple of inches below your belly button. It is the chakra that controls your emotions, which is why it correlates with your emotional body. This means that the sacral chakra relates to how your emotions and other people affect you. It is also in charge of creativity and sexual energy. An opened sacral chakra makes you feel in charge of your life. A blocked sacral chakra will make you feel like you lack control over your life, including your feelings and experiences. The sacral chakra's primary color is orange. Ultimately, this chakra affects everything centered around your feelings.

The third chakra is the Solar Plexus Chakra, which spiritualists also call the *Manipura.* The solar plexus chakra is found in the stomach area, around the upper abdomen area. This is the chakra that controls willpower and assertion. It symbolizes your confidence in taking charge of your life. An opened Solar Plexus chakra creates incredible feelings of self-confidence in you, but when this chakra is closed to the free flow of energy, it may cause intense anger, shame, frustration, and self-doubt. You may also feel like you are being victimized due to the lack of confidence in yourself. When your solar plexus chakra is open, you have the confidence to express your thoughts and feelings exactly as you experience them. You can reveal the true self. Since it is tied with self-confidence, this chakra also affects self-esteem and self-worth. The color is yellow.

The Heart Chakra is the fourth chakra in the chakra system. You may also call it the *Anahata.* The heart chakra is found in the center of the chest; it is the link between the upper and lower chakras. Basically, it is the middle chakra. Remember that the lower chakras are tied to the material realm, while the upper chakras are tied to the spiritual realm. This makes the heart chakra a link between materiality and spirituality. It helps you find a balance between the two. As you can probably tell from its name, the heart chakra dictates your ability to give love and receive in return, both from yourself and the surrounding people. When your heart chakra is blocked, you may find it challenging to open up about your feelings to the people in your life, but when this chakra is open, and the flow of energy is enabled, you will experience feelings of compassion and empathy. The heart chakra controls feelings of joy, love, and inner peace. The color of this chakra is green.

Next, you have the throat chakra, which is the fifth chakra. The throat chakra is also called the *Visuddha.* This chakra controls communication, truth, and self-expression. This means the throat chakra speaks to your ability to express yourself honestly and articulately. As evident from the name, this chakra is in the throat. Essentially, the fifth chakra speaks to what is in your heart. It influences your ability to communicate your true feelings and power. When the throat chakra is blocked, you might find it difficult to express your true feelings. A person whose throat chakra is blocked may have difficulty forming words that communicate how they feel about a person or a situation. But when the throat chakra is open to the free flow of energy, you can express yourself creatively, reliably, and truthfully. Blue is the color of the throat chakra.

The sixth chakra is the third-eye chakra, which you can also call *Ajna*. The higher you go up the chakra system, the closer you are to divine communication. Between your brows, the third-eye chakra is directly associated with intuition. It is your spiritual eye, which gives you the ability to see the bigger picture. The third-eye chakra influences your ability to access information that is not available at surface level. This chakra controls imagination, intuition, and wisdom. The third-eye chakra needs to be open to energy for you to learn and practice psychic abilities such as clairvoyance. You will learn more about this soon. It is not wrong to refer to the third-eye chakra as the eye of the soul because that is precisely what it is. When your third-eye chakra is open, you can see visions and know things intuitively. This chakra represents your ability to perceive and analyze truth in the physical and spiritual world. Purple is the color of the third-eye chakra.

The Crown Chakra is the final and seventh chakra in the chakra system. You may also call it the *Sahasrara*. As you can likely tell from the name, this chakra is at the crown at your head, meaning the very top of your head. It is atop your physical body. This chakra represents your connection with the spiritual and inner and outer beauty. It controls your ability to attain the highest spiritual connection. Only a few people can ever fully open their crown chakra to the life force flow. When the crown chakra becomes open, one reaches a state of higher consciousness ordinarily difficult to attain. The color of the crown chakra is white.

When you talk about things such as the aura, chakras, or nadis, the one thing at the center of all these things is energy. And that is why I say it all begins with energy. Psychic abilities from clairvoyance to clairsentience or telepathy are all about energy reading. Many people believe that only a few gifted people can sense and read energy. This is not correct.

Contrary to what you likely believe, energy reading is a skill, not a gift. As long as you put in the work and effort, you can harness the skills and read your energy and other people. Essentially, you now know that humans comprise energy, but most people fail to realize or acknowledge that all that energy needs to be directed somewhere. Suppose you are not mindful of the energy in and out of your body. There, it will all go to your head, resulting in overthinking, stress, and, ultimately, physical and emotional imbalance. When this happens, you become detached from your body and everything going on within it. Many diseases that the physical body suffers happen because of energy imbalance.

Let's look at an example. You have a car, and you know that your car requires a functional engine to work correctly. When your car malfunctions, it is easy to blame your engine for making the car malfunction. But when the engine has any problem, you know it. Now, being aware is one thing; taking actions to prevent the engine from collapsing is another thing. When you are aware and try to combat the brewing tragedy, you will prevent your car from breaking down. You must recognize when the engine has issues and then doing what you can to attend to it. This is precisely what it means to be mindful. Sensing/feeling your energy is the basis of mindfulness. Without this, you cannot keep your physical body, mind, and soul in a constant state of energy balance. Energy encapsulates everything in the universe. If you cannot feel the energy in your own body, you will be detached from the energy in the cosmic universe. And without the ability to feel the energy, it would be impossible to master or read energy. Basically, aura reading and other psychic abilities that revolve around energy would be impossible. So, how do you sense and feel energy?

To feel the energy, the first thing you must understand is that each person has their own unique experience with energy. You cannot feel the energy in the same way as the person next to you. Hence, there is no right or wrong way to sense or feel the energy. Your experience with energy is unique to you alone. Your vibrational frequency differs from that of others; the reality is whatever you see from your unique vantage position. There are limiting beliefs, blocks, and individual issues that come together to influence how you feel and read energy. Getting in tune with your energy is easy if you understand what to look for.

The first step to sensing your energy is to soften your awareness. Like all humans, you have a softness in you. To get across to this softness within you, you need a specific focus. You need to get rid of limiting blocks and boundaries. So, the first thing you must do is to focus on *yourself only.*

You must find time for yourself alone. Nobody will do this for you unless you do it yourself. Finding time for just yourself is something that you achieve through meditation. To sense or feel the energy, you must quiet your mind. Usually, the mind is a hectic place. It consists of different thoughts, feelings, memories, and visuals that can distract you. This mental chatter is akin to white noise for your mind; it makes it hard to focus on what is essential, which is yourself. You must quiet that mental chatter.

One method I find useful for getting rid of mental chatter is Jigam. Jigam is an ancient Korean word that literally translates to "stopping thoughts and emotions." Basically, you need to stop your thoughts and emotions to sense or feel the energy. Thankfully, Jigam is a super straightforward practice. Even if you have never practiced feeling energy before, you can sense energy with Jigam in under 60 seconds. Below are the steps to doing Jigam:

• Rap Your Fingers

Let your shoulders, wrists, and fingers relax. Then wrap the tip of your fingers against one another gently. This should feel like you are trying to wake your fingers up. Imagine a bird pecking and mimic the movement. Do this for 15 seconds.

• Wring or Twist Your Wrists Gently

Again, let your hands relax, holding both hands in an upright position. Then gently twist your wrists backward and forward. Do this as rapidly as possible while making sure that your hands remain in a relaxed state. Keep this up for 15 seconds. As you do this, breathe out any tension in your body.

• Bring Your Palms Close to Feel the Energy

While maintaining the relaxed feeling in your hand and wrist, gently bring your palms to face each other. Bring them close enough to feel the energy without letting them touch. Your palms should almost touch without actually touching. Now, concentrate on the middle of your palms, i.e., the space between both palms. Energy can be felt through heat, pulsating, or tingling. Immediately feel either of these sensations in the center of your palms. Maintain your focus for at least 15 seconds.

• Move the Energy

Once you feel the heat, tingling, or pulsating sensation between your palms, rotate your hands in a circular motion. Do this slowly. Then, gently pull your hands apart and push them closer again. As you do this, do not take your focus off the center of your palms. The energy sensation between your palms should become more substantial, bigger, and more transparent as you do this. You can keep moving the energy around for 10 to 15 seconds.

This simple exercise is beneficial for sensing and feeling your energy. Jigam is especially significant if you are the type who gets lost in your thoughts quite often. As you practice, you can sense the energy between your palms growing and growing. When you focus your mind on the sensation in your hands, you automatically redirect most of your mind's energy to your hand. This will naturally quieten the mental chatter going on in your head. Alternatively, you are also using your energy to maintain focus rather than your mind, as you would typically do. You will remain centered and grounded through the whole process, making it easy to do other psychic things.

Another thing to note about this exercise is that it increases the mindfulness of breathing. Although you may not realize it yet, breathing is vital to energy balance. These days, most people don't breathe beyond what they need to get them through each day. But focused or concentrated breathing improves how mindful you are of your body and energy. Focusing on your breathing does the same thing that meditation does. When you learn to put your mind and body in a relaxed state, you help your body (physical and spiritual) heal. Overload of mental chatter can make the body forget how to heal itself naturally.

Anybody can learn to read energy because it is a skill. The ability to read energy through the opening of the third-eye chakra is called clairvoyance. Although you can have the natural gift to "view" energy, you cannot be good at it unless you hone the skills. Without training your senses and other important aspects of energy reading, you may not have control over your clairvoyance. But clairsentience is the ability to feel the energy. While clairvoyants see energy, clairsentient can feel it. Clairsentients are also referred to as empaths or highly sensitive people.

Summarily, the energy system is one whole complex system without which your physical body cannot exist. The energy system comprises three vital components: the subtle energy bodies or the aura, the chakras or energy centers, and the nadis or the energy channels. These come together to give the body its material appearance and its full functionalities and capabilities.

In the next chapter, I talk in-depth about the anatomy of the aura. Without understanding aura anatomy, you cannot learn to sense or read your own aura and other people's.

Chapter Three: Aura Anatomy: The Seven Layers

As you have learned, your aura is a bubble of light surrounding you, from head to toe. What you haven't learned is that the aura is not just a single body. It comprises multiple layers, seven precisely. These layers interact and communicate information within the body through the chakra system or the energy centers, whichever you prefer. Each layer of your aura is associated with your physical, emotional, and spiritual state. Things such as your thoughts, emotions, wellbeing, awareness, life experiences, and energy vibrations are all stored in the layers of your auric field.

The seven layers of the aura are also called the subtle bodies. Each auric layer corresponds to one chakra or energy system. The form of the aura is achievable due to the energy that flows through the seven chakras. They also correspond with varying levels of human experiences. Depending on one's physical, emotional, and spiritual state, each layer of the aura can expand and contract at will. This means that some layers can look bigger or smaller than others, depending on your health and well-being.

Another thing to note is that they are made of different colors, representing different things, but at any point, there is usually one primary color that envelopes the largest part of the aura. This color can change depending on several factors you will learn more about.

Although the auric field isn't a single vibrational field, most people initially think it is hard to detect or see everyone's individual bodies. Even when you master the art of sensing and reading the aura, you might still struggle to see the seven subtle bodies. Fortunately, you don't have to see them before you can read or work with them. All you need is to learn how to sense the auric layers to start reading and interpreting them. Once you know the seven layers, working with them becomes easy. As a matter of fact, it becomes as easy as tuning into your emotions to sense and feel them. Tuning into your thought patterns as well as the physical state of your body also helps.

1st Layer: The Etheric Body

The etheric layer is the first subtle body; it is also the closest layer to the physical body. The etheric body is about 2 inches from the skin. This regulates the exchange of information between your body and your immediate environment. It is partly made of a bi-photonic field and a torsion field. This means that the etheric body gathers and distributes your vital life force from the sun and your environment. This layer is directly responsible for forming the shape of your physical body. It can be compared to the morphogenetic field, as explained in Rupert Sheldrake's theory. This is directly associated with your body's physical and material aspects. It deals with the awareness of the material plane. The etheric layer corresponds directly with the root chakra. Due to its proximity to the physical body, this layer is the densest of the seven subtle bodies, but the etheric body is of a vibrational level higher than the physical body, which is the lowest vibrational body.

As I have mentioned in an earlier chapter, the etheric field links your material body and the other subtle energy bodies. Typically, most people can't see the etheric layer even though it is the closest and most accessible to see due to its nearness to the material body. When you practice aura reading, this is the first subtle energy body you will see. At first, it will come to you as a grayish-white outline around the physical body. You will later see its color variants, with consistent practice, which range from bluish gray to brighter hues of blue or gray light. When the etheric layer is gray, this portrays a very active person. Blue, on the other hand, represents a more passive person. Due to its proximity to the material body, athletes and active people usually have more vital etheric layers than other people. This also is weaker in people who lead a more sedentary life.

The etheric layer is an energy matrix; its form is anchored to the material body. This is another reason it serves as the bridge between the physical body and the other higher bodies. The condition of your physical body reflects your etheric body's condition. Anything that happens to the physical body happens in the etheric layer first. Being in tune with your etheric layer and aura makes you aware of diseases and illnesses before they manifest in your physical body. Also, the etheric body can be affected by negative thoughts, feelings, and beliefs. The effects of these are typically physical ailments, tangles, disruptions, and breaks in the etheric layer.

By knowing and understanding how the etheric body interrelates with the other layers, you can master how to enhance every aspect of your life.

2nd Layer: The Emotional Body

The second layer of the auric field is called the emotional body. Sitting second from your physical body, this layer is linked with vibrational levels of your feelings. The emotional body is associated with the sacral chakra which is also associated with your emotional health and well-being. It is the layer where information about your feelings and emotions are stored. This layer is about one to three inches away from your physical body. Unlike the etheric layer, then this takes a fluid form, so it looks nothing like the physical body. Instead, it takes an oval shape looking like clouds of soft colors. The clouds appear to be in never-ending fluid movement, which stands for the full representation of your feelings and emotions. As your emotions change, these colors change. This expresses the moods you are in at different points. The emotional body contains all seven colors of the rainbow.

A piece of vital information to note that the emotional layer is that it strongly influences both the upper and lower layers of the auric field. Understanding the second layer is critical because of the profound influence it has on your health. Aura readers typically describe the emotional layer as having dark and cloudy areas representing the places where you experience pain and emotional blockage. Some of these areas are also stagnant, meaning they don't move in the same fluid way other areas of the emotional layer move. This second and some upper layers of the auric field can be perceived through the third-eye. It is also the point where you can quickly and clearly see most of the chakras.

When the emotional layer is blocked, you might experience problems with expressing your emotions and sexuality. The flow of energy in the emotional layer is usually communicated with the etheric layer. It then goes to the material body for processing. This means that when something happens in the emotional layer, the etheric layer gets wind of it and then manifests it in the physical body. So, when you experience physical tension or emotional pain, it is likely the result of the first layer receiving signals of the emotional blockage and pain happening in the second layer. When the emotional layer is open to energy flow, you will find it incredibly easy to express and communicate your emotions and sexuality.

Several negative things happen when you harbor negative beliefs and emotions in the second layer. First, you might experience blocks of energy to other auric layers. These blockages are usually dark. You might also have to deal with stagnated energy, so all your energy will be concentrated in one place instead of flowing freely through your seven chakras. This can affect your physical and mental health. Another effect it can have is depleted energy, meaning you will burn out faster than usual. This can leave you feeling generally weaker and incapable.

It is vital to ensure that the emotional layer is always healthy and vibrant to affect other layers negatively.

3rd Layer: The Mental Body

The third subtle energy body of the auric field is the mental layer or mental body. As you can probably tell from its name, the mental layer is the energy body linked with your thoughts and mental processes. This third auric layer is connected to the Solar Plexus chakra. As I already said, this is the chakra that concerns your personal power. The third auric layer is associated with your ego and personal power. The mental layer comprises a finer and brighter substance than that of the emotional layer. This auric layer typically appears in the form of a bright and shiny yellow light that illuminates your head and shoulders, hanging just around your whole body. This means that yellow is the color that represents your mind and your intellect.

The yellow light of the mental layer pulsates and shines brighter when a person focuses on tasks that require their mental strength. Also, the mental layer hangs about 3 to 8 inches away from the physical body. The third layer comprises the structure of your thoughts and ideas. You can see your linear thinking processes and how your thoughts form when you look at the mental layer. The stronger your thought forms are, the more defined they appear in your mental body. It is vital that you have a profound and in-depth knowledge of your mental layer. This, as you will find, will be to your advantage as an aura reader.

Your thoughts have colors just as your emotions do. As a matter of fact, the color expressed by your thought-forms in the mental layer reflects the true nature of the feelings attached to these thoughts. Note that the three lower auric layers are directly connected with how things, such as diseases and illnesses, manifest in the material body. Things such as unwanted thoughts, negative beliefs, and others are all part of what makes up your personality. This means that your mental layer is affected by things that happen in the three lower auric layers. When it is out of balance, it typically affects clarity in thinking. This means that you may not be able to process your thoughts as you should. When this happens, it inadvertently affects your ability to express yourself and your feelings. Again, this goes back to the connection between the colors of the mental layer and the emotional layer's colors. Negative belief in the mental layer can cause the dissociation of an individual's thought forms and the disturbance of the mental layer's form.

The best way to ensure that your clarity of thinking is never out of balance is by learning how to balance your aura. When the aura is in great shape, all the auric layers will remain in a state of balance, ensuring vitality for the physical body.

4th Layer: The Astral Body

The fourth auric layer is the astral body, which can also be called the spiritual body. Connected with the heart chakra, the astral body is associated with things that concern physical, mental, and emotional expression. Your astral body is the link between the physical plane and the spiritual plane(s). This means it also connects your three higher auric layers with the three remaining three lower auric layers, just as the heart chakra is the bridge between the upper and lower chakras. The astral layer is also called the bridge layer because of this.

All energy must pass through the astral body when going from the spiritual plane to the physical plane and vice versa. Without the astral body, it would be impossible for humans to travel the astral plane and interact with higher or spiritual beings. Basically, all forms of healing energy pass through the astral layer. The astral body is considered the first spiritual layer; it is where love exists, both on a specific and universal level.

The astral body comprises clouds of multiple colors, plus it is of an amorphous nature. This means it exists without a definite shape, unlike the physical body. The astral layer extends about 1 to 1 ½ feet from the material body. Being the bridge between the physical and spiritual planes, this is a crucial part of the energy body. Without the astral layer, you simply cannot connect with the higher dimensions of reality. You also cannot visit the astral plane unless you project your astral form.

Due to its direct connection with the heart chakra, the astral layer requires strong, intimate relationships to maintain its strength. In fact, reliable, intimate relationships make the astral layer stronger. This also means that the astral body can become weaker when you experience conflicts with your loved ones. For instance, breaking up with a partner can make the astral layer weaker than usual. When you have an intimate relational bond with your loved ones, the astral body's colors become brighter and more vibrant, radiating stronger than ever. When you have a codependent and loveless bond with loved ones, the astral layer's colors become weak and dull, dimming moment by moment. The colors can also be affected when the heart chakra is weak and blocked to vital energy flow. As the bridge between the chakras, you can easily access all seven chakras from your astral layer.

The quality of your astral body usually reflects how spiritually developed you are. The higher your level of spiritual awareness and development, the healthier your astral body will be. Being spiritually developed and aware also makes it easier to gain access to the astral plane and other spiritual planes. If you are spiritually underdeveloped, your astral body will probably be diminutive, small, and cloudy. But being spiritually advances give you a strong, clear, and expanded astral form.

5th Layer: The Etheric Template

The etheric template is the fifth auric layer and is directly related to the fifth chakra. This auric layer is home to the energetic blueprint of everything on the physical plane; that's why it is called the *etheric template*. It comprises the matrix where your physical body took shape. Typically, the etheric template creates a negative space that creates a structure from which the physical body is formed. Just as the throat chakra is connected to, the etheric template is the auric layer that brings everything to life on the physical plane. The etheric template is precisely the part of the aura where illnesses and diseases can be detected before their manifestation in your physical body. The etheric template is also where healing can begin. This layer of the aura can take on various colors due to the negative space it creates. The etheric template often appears like the negative of a photograph to those who see it. The vibrational level in the fifth layer is where sound creates living matter. The etheric template typically extends about 1 ½ to 2 feet from the physical body. It is also usually more structured than some other auric layers.

For balance and restoration to occur in the etheric body, which is the first layer and the densest layer after the physical body, this must first happen in the etheric template. The etheric layer and the physical body cannot be free from illnesses and diseases unless the etheric template is free. Healing happens faster and more effectively in the etheric template. This is because the fifth layer reflects how the aura portrays your physical health, mental activity, emotional state, and character on a higher vibrational level. When you visit the higher plane, you can always know when diseases form in the etheric template.

An out-of-balance etheric template often affects the energy system. When the fifth auric layer is dysfunctional, it often results in a free fall of the whole energy system. Thus, it is essential to ensure that your fifth layer never becomes unbalanced or out-of-shape. When you become free from worldly limitations, the etheric template tends to shine brighter and healthier. This also happens when you learn to express yourself originally and authentically.

6th Layer: The Celestial Body

Also called the causal body, the celestial body is the sixth layer of the auric field. In simple terms, the celestial layer is the place where spiritual connection and enlightenment begins. This is because of its direct connection with the third-eye chakra and why it is sometimes called the intuitive level. It is your loving connection with all other beings in existence and is also one of the strongest auric layers. The celestial layer comprises light exclusively. This layer is where you can attain higher levels of thoughts, feelings, and manifestations. It is also where you can attain *spiritual ecstasy.*

The celestial layer is the part of the aura where you can connect with the Higher Being, "God," "The All That Is," or anything else you call that level of existence. It is the place of unconditional love flow. This sixth layer extends about 2 to 3 feet from the physical body. Unlike many of the auric layers, it is typically harder to see when reading the aura. Since it is made exclusively of light, the celestial layer's colors appear in beautiful, shiny light. The colors typically comprise pastel colors, which is why some spiritually inclined people love to call the celestial layer's colors the "mother-of-pearl." The light of the celestial layer also has a gold-silver shimmer, and the quality is beautifully opalescent.

Learning about the sixth auric layer and fully understanding its existence can expand your awareness and open your mind to the different dimensions of existence. The celestial layer contains accurate information about your past, present, and future life. An understanding of this energy field layer gives you unrestricted access to real accounts about your life. When you practice and become in tune with your intuitive senses or become closely connected to the spirit planes, the colors of your celestial body will shine more brightly and powerfully. It also becomes stronger when you learn to channel spiritual messages and guidance. Through meditation and devotional spiritual practices, you can easily connect your physical mind with the celestial layer's spiritual mind.

The celestial auric layer is home to memories, dreams, intuitive knowledge, trust, honesty, spiritual awareness, and unconditional love. It is truly the place where you can experience what it is like to be part of something greater than yourself. A strong celestial layer gives you the ability to interact and receive messages from angels and other beings in the spirit world. When it is weak, you may find it difficult to connect or communicate with the spirit world.

Healing the celestial layer requires unconditional love.

7th Layer: The Ketheric Template

The *Ketheric template* is the seventh and final layer of the auric field. It is often regarded as the mental level of the spiritual world. This layer is the farthest layer from the physical body and the material plane, so it is also the closest to the spiritual plane. The Ketheric template is directly connected to your crown chakra, which, as you have learned, sits at the very top of your head, just outside your physical body. This layer extends about 2 ½ to 3 feet from the physical body. Just as the etheric template is the blueprint for the physical body, the Ketheric template is the spiritual structure's blueprint. It provides a negative space from which your spiritual awareness is formed.

The seventh layer is directly connected to the Universal Consciousness, which you may call *the Divine*. It has all the plans about your life, including your soul contract. It is also home to all the experiences and events that your soul has experienced and will experience. This layer also contains karma, programs, and patterning; basically, everything that affects and impacts your soul regardless of the time in which it is existing.

The Ketheric template comprises tiny, glowing silver threads that hold all the other auric layers and chakras together. Basically, this layer surrounds all the other auric layers. Together, these form the interconnection and interface between you and every other thing. This auric layer is of golden color and pulsates rapidly at a consistent rate. It also vibrates at a higher vibrational frequency than all the other layers. You need to unlock the Ketheric template to become one with the Divine and the universe. When the Ketheric layer is unlocked, you achieve a deeper understanding of the structure and order of the cosmic/universe, and the place you hold within it. You also gain the ability to tap into your Akashic records and access information about your past life and memories and anybody else's.

The Ketheric template is also connected with your belief systems. Naturally, you form your belief systems from the things you see, observe, and practice. Through your Ketheric template, you can tap into the auric layers and chakra associated with beliefs and form experiences that transform negative beliefs to positive ones. It is easy to form positive beliefs in the replacement of negative ones. You can turn "I'm fat" to "I'm beautiful." When you embrace certain beliefs, you can make them come true for you. As your beliefs shift from negative to positive, you are going through spiritual evolvement and development.

A vital thing to note about the Ketheric template is that you cannot experience its awesomeness while consumed by the ego. Your ego gives you a limiting view of issues. You need to overcome its limitations to experience the Ketheric template and become one with the Divine.

All seven layers discussed above may be regarded as distinct, individual bodies. But they interconnect and intermingle with one another based on your daily experiences. One fact highly misunderstood about the auric layers is that you need not see the layers to work with the aura. You need only to close your eyes and tune in to your aura. By only doing this, you can gain access to a wholesome amount of information and knowledge about your auric field and the state of each of your auric layers.

Soon, you will learn how you can feel into auras for readings.

Chapter Four: Perceiving Your Own Aura

To perceive your aura, you must begin with energy. That is why the second chapter is titled "*It All Starts with Energy.*" Without learning to perceive your own energy, you can't learn to sense or see the aura. After all, your aura is your human energy field. Basically, when you learn to perceive energy, perceiving your aura becomes easier than you can imagine. Remember that Jigam exercise I explained in the energy chapter? That exercise is highly essential to start sensing and reading your own energy levels.

Sensing your aura is only the beginning. The harder you practice, the sooner you can see and interpret the auras of people around you. Fortunately, perceiving your own aura isn't as hard as you probably have in mind. You, or anybody else, can learn to see the aura. You need not possess psychic abilities or powers to see the aura, but having psychic abilities potentially makes you more potent at seeing auras than others. Also, learning and practicing aura sensing is one of the best ways to hone and develop the dormant intuitive gifts you may not know you have. As I have mentioned, one can either see or feel auras. Seeing the aura is one thing; feeling it is another thing. It all depends on whether you are a clairvoyant or a clairsentient person.

The way you perceive energy is inherently different from how another person will perceive it. To sense your subtle energy bodies, you must understand what works for you. Some people feel the energy with their hands. Some can actually see it. Some have a sense of "knowing" it. Some can sense simply sense it. Some smell it. Others get a sensation like tasting. These are all forms of perception. What they tell you is that the way people perceive energy is different. How you perceive your aura is unique to you. And that is why "perceive," not "feel" or "see" is the keyword in the chapter title. There is no right or wrong way to perceive energy. More important, there is no specific way that is better than others. Some methods may be faster and quicker than others, but that is just about it. Being faster or quicker doesn't make them better or more effective than other ways of exception. That is precisely why you must work on knowing and embracing how works better for you.

I should also note you can perceive different things when trying to see, feel, or sense your aura or that of any other person. It doesn't mean you are doing it in a wrong or right way. There are so many channels to tune into when you want to perceive your aura. You may tune into one channel this time and tune into another channel when you do it a second time. This means you may get different kinds of information about yourself, depending on the energy channel you tune into at a particular point.

As humans, we perceive energy frequently. Since we are essentially made up of energy, this is a never-ending process for us. The problem lies in our awareness of the energy's existence. Unfortunately, most people rarely have a conscious awareness of their energy or aura. For example, you can meet someone new and immediately dislike them without even knowing their name or anything else. This results from an auric phenomenon. Perceiving aura is something you already do on a subconscious level, even if you may not realize it. You sense your own energy, and you sense that of other people. You do this naturally. But to learn of your aura, you need to pay attention to the subtle vibes you get about yourself and other people. More than you know, your body is a powerful and mostly accurate aura reader. Therefore, some people make you feel naturally relaxed and happy, while others make you feel instantly anxious and tense. When things like these happen, that is your body's aura reading abilities at work. Your body is basically reading their energy and informing you on a subconscious level. Most times, when your body reads someone's energy, and you feel a way about them, you don't know why you are feeling that way about them. This is because you are not consciously in tune with your own aura. Consciously tuning in with your aura will give you insight into the energy or vibe you get from the people you meet, old or new.

As I stated earlier, perceiving your aura doesn't require you to be psychic. You may have already felt or seen your own aura or that of another person before. If you have ever been emotionally affected in the presence of another person in a way you don't understand, then you have experienced what it feels like to perceive auras. If you are a kinesthetic person, you are more likely to perceive auras through "feeling." This makes you a clairsentient – someone who can feel things beyond the physical or material realm.

But if you are a visual person, you are more likely to perceive auras through "seeing." This makes you a clairvoyant – someone with the ability to see things beyond the material plane. Your hands are the most comfortable means for feeling your aura if you are kinesthetic.

Why Do You Need to Perceive Auras?

The aura is an extraordinary element. The colors and intensity of your aura have a profound and unique meaning. When you perceive and observe your aura, you can gain insight into certain things you don't know about yourself yet. Perceiving other people's auras also gives you knowledge of their thoughts and feelings before they are expressed verbally. If a person lies to you, you can tell through your perception of their aura. Unless you allow them, no one can lie to you undetected. The aura reflects everyone's true nature and intentions.

Also, the aura is your spiritual signature. When you see your aura, and it's bright and clean, you are physically and spiritually healthy. If you see this in another person, you can be sure of the same thing, even though they may not know this. And when you check your aura, and it's dark and broody, you can sense that they are not spiritually advanced. They may also not have good intentions towards you. Regardless of how impressive, educated, or good-meaning a person may appear physically, their aura will always reveal their true nature to you.

Learning to perceive and read auras also gives you awareness of dysfunctions and diseases long before they manifest in the physical body. Being conscious of your aura gives you the ability to heal yourself in the auric field before your physical form even shows illness or sickness symptoms, but what you can achieve through understanding your aura goes way beyond the healing of your physical body. Perceiving, observing, and interpreting your aura can help your consciousness in ways you won't understand until you reap these benefits. Conscious awareness and understanding of your aura can result in significant spiritual development and vast cosmic awareness.

Everyone on earth may have an aura, but the fact remains that most people have dull and weak auras. You may have a weak and dull aura too. You can tell when you practice seeing, feeling, or sensing your aura. If you find you have a weak and dull aura, it may result from a materialistic attitude, which is unsurprisingly common with humans. It could also be the consequence of negating and suppressing your consciousness' development, and cultivating negative emotions such as fear, anger, jealousy, and envy. Negative emotions generally suppress your true nature, which inadvertently means that your aura is suppressed too.

When you perceive your aura, you may be shocked to find something that isn't encouraging. This may happen when you try to see other people's auras too. You may also see something that you don't understand. Reasons like these are why it is essential to perceive your own aura yourself and learn to interpret whatever you see yourself. Learning to perceive your own aura also allows you to improve it. When you see your aura and don't like or understand what you see, you will learn to cleanse, heal, and do other necessary things to improve your aura's appearance to others. Ultimately, you can dictate what they see about your thoughts and feelings. In that process, you are setting yourself on the path to becoming a wiser and better version of yourself. If you think about it, the world will become a better place if everyone could see and read each other's auras. We would all work on improving our auras, which would simultaneously improve the cosmic energy.

Having understood how energy and aura perception works and why it is crucial to perceive auras, also understand that several exercises can be used to start perceiving your own aura and energy. Again, remember that the Jigam exercise in Chapter 2 is all about how you can quieten your mental chatter to prepare yourself to perceive auras in any way that works for you. As it usually is with people with one psychic ability or the other, you can see an aura spontaneously or otherwise. In this context, otherwise means deliberately or at will. While it can be fun and exciting to see auras spontaneously, it is better to learn how to perceive your aura at will. To deliberately initiate a clairvoyance or clairsentient experience, the first thing to do is find your trigger. You also need to learn how to stimulate situations that make it easier to operate your trigger.

This is where aura reading techniques come in. There are several simple and advanced techniques you can use on your own to trigger clairvoyance or clairsentience. When you master these techniques, there would be no further need to create and follow schedules as to when you perceive your aura and when you don't. This also applies to aura reading with other people. Mastering these techniques and exercises means you can trigger yourself at 3 AM or 3 PM in the evening; essentially, you can perceive your aura whenever you want.

Below are specific basic and advanced exercises very effective for perceiving your own aura, whether you are a clairvoyant or a clairsentient individual.

Clairvoyance: Perceiving Your Aura Through Your Eyes

To practice your clairvoyance exercises, you need to first learn to put your physical body in a relaxed state. You also need to learn with your chi energy to enhance your ability to see your aura. Putting your physical body in a relaxed state makes it easier for you to see and identify perceptions from your auric field and your subtle energy bodies. Relaxation is a critical part of clairvoyance practice and development. Remember that your energy is the only thing that can connect your subtle bodies to your physical body in the material plane. To an extent, the energy body is the glue between the astral and the physical planes.

As a rule of thumb, it is much easier to achieve visual or psychic perceptions generally when your energy field is expanded, and your astral body is a little less bound to your physical body. When this happens, you may feel like your body is rocking from side to side, even though no physical movement exists. In this process, you may even feel a pleasurable floating sensation in your hands and body, too. When this happens, it is called the *misalignment of vehicles.* When you are in this state, you may find that your extra physical senses are more alert and active. This is because your astral body is moving around subtly, without you realizing it. To reach the misalignment of vehicle state, you need to achieve a physical relaxation state first. You can do this through meditation and energy work.

Below is an easy-to-do meditation technique to ease your body into a relaxed state and prepare it for the clairvoyance exercise.

Breathing Exercise

Focused breathing is one of the easiest ways to relax your physical body meditatively.

- Wear something light and comfortable. Find a quiet environment to relax your body. Don't forget you can do the Jigam to quieten the noise in your head before you begin.

- Sit on a comfortable chair or on the floor, whichever you find comfortable enough for the breathing exercise.

- Do the Jigam exercise to reduce the busy events happening in your head to the barest minimum. Now, focus your awareness on the rise and fall of your breath. Do not attempt to change the rhythm of your breathing. Simply focus on the breathing itself.

- Feel as they move in and out of your lungs. Focus on the sensations this produces throughout your body.

- You may notice that your breathing is becoming slower, gentler, more resonant, softer, and more even. If not, don't pay mind to this. Keep the focus on your breath. Eventually, you will get to that stage where your breaths are gentler, softer, and more even.

For most people, it is usually more difficult than usual to focus entirely on your breath. Naturally, your attention will wander to other things. You may even catch yourself thinking about some other issues. Don't be alarmed or regretful, as this is quite normal. Do not judge yourself for letting your mind wander. When you notice that your attention has shifted, gently bring your mind back to your thoughts. Pay attention to the gap between the thoughts and do your best to expand that gap.

Eventually, you will feel the tension in your body evaporate. You will also notice as your physical body gently and calmly enters a relaxed state, which could last the whole day if the exercise is done right. Do the breathing exercise for at least 5 minutes. Once you are confident that your body is relaxed, you can proceed to the next exercise.

Third-Eye Chakra Activation Exercise

Remember that the third-eye chakra is the chakra that is directly connected to intuition. Without activating your third-eye chakra, you cannot visually perceive your aura or that of any other person. This exercise will help you activate your third-eye chakra so clairvoyance becomes possible for you.

- Lie down and make yourself comfortable. Consider resting your head on a stack of pillows to where you can see the tip of your feet while your eyes remain relaxed. Ensure that your eyes don't feel strained, and you don't have to look up or down before you can see the tip of your feet in that position. Make sure that the lights in the room you are using are off. The room shouldn't be totally dark; make sure there are minimal streams of light.

- Try to maintain the relaxed state you achieved through the breathing exercise by keeping your eyes closed and resting for up to 10 minutes. You can set a timer to ensure that you don't go beyond 10 minutes, but make sure that your timer's sound isn't jarring enough to take you out of your meditative state. Also, keep the timer close to you so you won't have to move your body too much when you reach out to switch it off.

- Now, tune into your auric field – and the chakras in particular.

- Focus on the third-eye chakra, i.e., the chakra between in the space between your eyebrows. Keep your eyes closed. Gather your energies through your chakras and focus the energy on the third-eye chakra for at least 10 seconds. Then, materialize the gathered energy in a particularly strong flow force for up to three seconds. The gathered and materialized energies are from your subtle energy bodies.

- Try to make the energy extend about one meter from the place where you have your third-eye chakra. Pause for three seconds. Then, repeat this action: gather, then materialize energies from your subtle energy bodies. Repeat this action twenty times.

As you engage in this exercise, you may experience sensations such as tingling, bubbling, and pressure in your forehead. These are three sensations that people typically experience when activating the third-eye chakra to see their aura, but there are tons of other sensations that people generally report experiencing. What you experience may be unique to you, so I recommend taking notes after you are done to identify and label the sensation patterns you experience during this exercise. Usually, when you experience these sensations, it means that your third-eye chakra is activating and opening. Once it is opened, you can do the next exercise to see your own aura.

Seeing Your Own Aura

Once you have activated your third-eye chakra, seeing your aura is just a few steps away. With the steps below, you can see the energies coursing through your energy centers and channels. Basically, you can see your aura and even glance into your energy field.

- Gently open your closed eyes and look over the tip of your feet.

- Focus your sight on the tip of your toes throughout and don't move your body. This is to avoid bringing your body out of the relaxed and activated state. Also avoid blinking. If you must blink, do it as gently as possible. Some aura readers try to shut their eyes partially to avoid blinking too rapidly.

- Gently try to change your view's focal point to multiple points along the linear gap between your toes and your gaze. Ensure that you do this without moving or blinking, if possible. It should feel as if you are trying to look at dust speckles on that point.

You should slowly see a bright color contour around your feet or some other part of your body when you do this. There, you see your aura! You may also see colors around your chest and waist. These are all areas of your aura. Initially, you may only see the lower layers of your auric field. But with time and practice, you can see the higher layers of your auric field.

Below is another effective exercise for seeing your aura. This exercise is fast and efficient. Using this exercise, most people can see their auras within five minutes. For this exercise, too, make sure that the room has a white wall. It should also be quiet, and light is low. Note that your eyes need to switch to night vision.

- Start by sitting across a part of the white wall. Support yourself with a comfortable chair and gently firm your feet flatly against the ground. Use this period to practice the Jigam and breathing exercise for mental and physical relaxation.

- Next, extend one of your arms, with your palm facing the white wall and your fingers close together. Gently relax your gaze as you look at your extended hand. Maintain the softened gaze for at least 30 seconds. You should instantly start to see the energy field around your hand.

- In slow motion spread your fingers slowly. Do not stop looking softly at the fingers and the space between them. At this point, you should start seeing an outline of your aura.

- With consistency in time and practice, you will start seeing an outline of your aura around your hand, your fingers and the spaces between. Initially, it may appear to you as a colorless heatwave. With time, you will start seeing the different colors that make up your auric field.

The more you practice, the better you will get at doing this in different light conditions without needing a white background.

If you would prefer much simpler techniques for seeing your own aura, below are other quick exercises you can use. You can try these advanced and straightforward exercises until you figure out the ones that work the best for you personally.

Simple Exercise 1

- This is for when you want to see the aura around your hand. You will need your hand, a white piece of paper, and a room with natural lighting for this exercise.

- Gently place your palm on the white paper and spread your fingers apart. Make sure that your palm is facing downwards. Do not spread your fingers apart too much. Relax your body and be comfortable.

- Focus your gaze on your hand, but don't do this directly – your gaze should be on the spaces between your fingers. Also, take your eyes out of focus. You may feel strange the first time you do this.

- Maintain your gaze, and quickly, you will start seeing the glow of your aura around your fingers. When that happens, you see your etheric layer, which, as I have said, is the first layer of your aura and the easiest to see.

Simple Exercise 2

This exercise will help you see the aura around your whole body. To do it, you need a mirror and yourself. When trying this exercise, it is best to use the daylight so you need not switch on your bathroom lights. This is to ensure that the bathroom lights don't enter your eyes while you focus on seeing your aura. Plus, leaving the lights off makes the atmosphere relaxing for you.

- Stand in front of your mirror. Before this, you should have done the relaxing exercise to make yourself comfortable and relaxed.

- You need only to look at your reflection in the mirror. As weird as this may sound, take note you won't be looking directly at yourself in the mirror.

- Ensure that your eyes are out of focus as this makes your aura appear to you more easily. Specifically, focus above the tips of your fingers and let your vision go out of focus a little.

- Soften your gaze as you do this.

Even though this exercise is simple and straightforward, you may need a lot of practice to get it right. You won't start seeing colors right away. So, don't be disheartened if the colors don't come as fast as you expect.

I always tell people who want to see their auras there are ways you can make your aura appear to you faster than you think is possible. To see your aura or that of any other person, you have to increase your eyes' sensitivity. Then, you need to widen the range of perceptible vibration beyond the visible light. You need to take your vision out of focus. To achieve the out-of-focus look, you must train your peripheral vision. Using your peripheral vision makes it easier to see your aura. You are wondering how this is possible.

Your retina is the part of your eye responsible for focus. It also contains photosensitive cells. The retina is less damaged in the peripheral vision than when your vision is in the central part. The central part of your retina is the most used part of the retina; it is always used for everyone. It has accumulated a lot of damage over the years of usage. This damage comes from years of excessive and artificial illumination from your computers, phones, TVs, and artificial lights. Also, humans have generally trained their central vision to be utilized in different ways since inception. This is why it is easier for younger children to see auras – because their central vision is still in an excellent or almost-perfect condition. Once children start maturing to the age where they begin school, they tend to learn to use their vision differently. Consequently, they start losing their natural auric sight.

Another way to increase the sensitivity of your eyes is to increase exposure. When you want to shoot photos in a dark scene with your camera, you must increase the camera's film's exposure. To achieve this with your eyes, you only need to concentrate on ONE specific spot in your environment for about 30 to 60 seconds. When your eyes move or something moves in front of your eyes, they immediately average the images. When you concentrate on one spot for at least 30 seconds, you increase your sensitivity because the incoming light becomes average. This cumulates the effects of that light. Concentration exercises are efficient for increasing exposure and increasing the sensitivity of your eyes.

Clairsentience: Perceiving Your Aura by Feeling

Clairsentience, as I defined before, is the psychic ability which entails feeling and perceiving things beyond the physical or material realm. When you "feel" your aura instead of seeing it, this is known as clairsentience. If you can't work on seeing your aura through your visual sense, it doesn't matter if you can feel or perceive it. As you have learned, there is more than one way to perceive the aura; it doesn't have to be through clairvoyance. If you are kinesthetic, you are better off trying the exercises under this subheading to perceive your own aura.

The hands are the primary and most comfortable means for feeling your aura. To perceive your aura through feeling, you need to do the relaxation exercise first. Also, you need to be in a quiet area where there will be no interruptions throughout the clairsentience exercises. These are all essential requirements to remember for your practice sessions.

How to Feel Your Aura

- Start by sitting comfortably on the chair or floor. If you are sitting on a chair, make sure there is something to support your back. Ground your feet firmly on the ground.

- Close your eyes softly and tune in with your breath. Feel as your breath enters your body, moves through it, and then leave it. Focus on the movement of your breath in and out of your body for 1 to 2 minutes.

- With your eyes still closed, rub your palms against each other briskly. This should last for 20 to 30 seconds.

- Spread your hands in front of you, with the elbows bent slightly and your palms facing each other. The distance between both palms should be about one foot apart.

- Slowly, move your hands towards each other. Do this without making them touch.

- Again, slowly move your hands apart. Do this slowly and focus on the sensations you are getting. You should start feeling something in the space between your palms.

- Do the above process repeatedly – slowly bring your hands closer and draw them apart slowly again.

- Your eyes should remain closed as you repeat these steps. If you feel yourself getting distracted, tune in with the movement of your breath again. Observe as your breath enters your body, moves through it, and then leaves the body again. This will help you stay grounded, leaving your attention stabilized and keeping distractions far away from you.

- Continue the process of drawing your hands apart and bringing them closer again. Focus on any sensation, thought, and image that come to your mind in these moments. Focus on whatever you are sensing in the space between your palms as you bring them almost together and draw them apart again.

- What changes occur to the sensation when the distance between your palms change? Observe this as you practice.

Remember that you have no right or wrong way to go about this exercise. Everything you experience at that moment is your own reality, and your reality is unique to you and you are alone. It is how you perceive the energy of the subtle bodies of your aura.

As you practice this clairsentience exercise, you can eventually see your energy field with your eyes wide open. Practice the "feeling" exercise if you can't immediately get yourself to perceive your aura visually. The more you practice, the closer you will get to seeing your aura with your eyes.

Perceiving your own aura requires dedicating enough time to practice. As the saying goes, practice makes perfect. The more practice you put in, the better you will get at seeing your own energy field, and that of others. The takeaway from this chapter is that you can learn to see auras; in fact, anyone can. So, don't be disheartened or discouraged if your aura doesn't immediately come to you. If you can't see your aura, you can sense or feel it. This takes nothing away from you.

There are different ways to perceive your own aura – find the method that works best for you. Don't forget to have fun while you are at it!

Chapter Five: How to See Human Auras

Seeing human auras is relatively easy. All the techniques we have discussed above can be used for seeing other people, with some tweaks here and there. One thing about aura-seeing techniques is that you only need about one minute to learn them. But mastery usually takes a while. You may take years to see people's auras enough to acquire the information and make vital interpretations.

Seeing human auras requires patience. Without patience, most people give up on their dreams of becoming prolific aura readers. You may see people's auras the first time you try. Sometimes, you may take a few days of intense practice to see them. You may also not get the grasp of it in days of practice. There are also instances where one sees auras immediately and then stops seeing anything during a specific period which may be lengthy or not. Although you may see colors immediately once you practice seeing people's auras; some people need to practice for several months before they see colors. So, don't be alarmed if you fall into this category. Even if you see colors when you perceive your own energy field, it doesn't mean you will see colors when you practice with someone other than yourself. Seeing human auras is much easier when you have clean and open chakras. Blocked chakras make clairvoyance and clairsentience harder than they should be.

As with all psychic abilities, seeing human auras means you shouldn't strain or overwork yourself. When you begin, you should only practice for a few minutes each day. As you practice, you will get better at refocusing, and your eyes will become used to refocusing. This will enable you to look at auras for a more extended period. If your chakras become strained due to practice, it is better to stop practicing for a few days. In that few days of no practice, work on cleansing and healing your chakras before you practice again. This applied to every time you overwork and strained your chakras.

Exercise 1: Seeing Human Auras

You need a partner to work with. Get your partner to stand in front of a mirror. Remember that it is best to work in a room with a white and black background. The person you are working with should stand about 18 inches from the white background. To see the person's auras, you need to look behind the person, i.e., the black and white wall. Your eyes should be a few inches away from their body. If you still remember, there were 3D stereogram pictures that used to be popular a few years ago. With the 3D stereogram pictures, one had to look a couple of inches into the stereo "noise" to see the image. This trick applies to see the practice person's aura too. The concept applies to auras.

You need to look beyond the area where the person is standing. Do not look directly at their body; if you do, you may lose the aura's outlined image. Instead, focus on the area surrounding them where their white background looks lighter than other areas. Try to see if there are colors. If you could pick a specific color to describe that area with, what would that color be? Also, remembering that the auric layers comprise different colors, the color you describe one area that may differ from the rest. Once the color (s) appear to you, make it sway from side to side. The aura you are looking at should move with the movement you try. Any after-image rarely moves with the real person; it only moves when you move your eyes. Afterimages are the opposite color of what appears you are looking at; auras are of any color.

This technique allows you to practice seeing the different colors of the aura by looking at the afterimages. To do this, get colored construction paper or plain paper and color them with different colored markers. You should have red, yellow, orange, green, purple, blue, pink, white, and black colors. Now, cut out circles around 3 inches in diameter from the colored papers and place one of the colored circles on a white paper. Focus on it for 20 to 30 seconds and then remove the colored circle and focus on the white paper. An after-image should appear to you, and it should be the direct opposite of the colored paper you just stared at. Bring that color into your focus, and your eyes should refocus a couple of inches deeper than the surface of the white paper. It should feel as if you are looking at auras. Practice this process with each of the colored circles.

For most people, seeing the whitish glow that usually appears first isn't exactly a problem. So, this is what you will see when you practice. After a few days or months of practice, that whitish glow may have blue, yellow, and pink layers. With more practice, the colors will break down even further. The yellow may show a hint of orange and the green with a new light blue layer. The etheric body is usually the first layer of the aura to become visible to the ordinary eye. It is vivid, so you should start seeing it after a few months of diligent practice. Even when you can see no specific colors in the energy field, you will see the etheric field. Eventually, you may even see people's chakras, which are usually brighter.

If you are a student and regularly go to school, you can practice seeing human auras with your classmates and teachers. At work, you can look at your coworkers' auras when they are talking to you or doing something that allows you to practice. The more chances you have at practicing human auras in abstract environments, the more you will improve at seeing auras. But be careful not to stare while looking at people's auras without their knowledge. Be as discreet as possible.

Exercise 2: Seeing Human Auras

The exercise above isn't the only one you can use to see human auras. Again, you need to work with someone you know, a partner. After practicing with this person, you can also work with other people. Here are the steps below.

- Ask the person you are practicing with to stand 10 to 12 feet away from you. You can have a background either white or black. Adjust the lighting in the room so it isn't too bright or too dim. The best thing you can do is practice with natural lighting.

- Focus on the person's nose. Do not strain your eyes in the bid to focus. Your gaze should be soft and relaxed, enabling you to also use your peripheral vision to focus. The good thing about human vision is in its circularity. Even when you focus on the bridge of a person's nose, you can also look at their sides with your peripheral vision.

- You should see a gray and shadowy outline appear around the person's body. This outline should look benign and not thick. Avoid getting over-excited to where you take your focus away from the nose to the shadowy figure. Be relaxed.

- Using your peripheral vision, watch the outline around the person's figure. As you observe, their aura will take form before your eyes.

- Lift your gaze from their nose to their forehead. Be gentle and still when you do this. It will enable you to see the aura more clearly.

Initially, you may see a one-colored aura when you start practicing. But with time, you will start seeing the different colors in that person's aura.

This technique requires a lot of patience, practice, and concentration. You may have to put in a lot of time before you get it right, but you also may not take any time at all. Sometimes, your level of concentration makes all the difference. It also depends on how you channel your consciousness and yourself as a whole. Initially, take note that the aura will disappear whenever you blink while practicing. This is due to your brain shutting what you were looking at peripherally before you blinked. But as you practice more and more, this will cease to happen.

Exercise 3: Seeing Human Auras

Sometimes, the best way to see human auras is to practice sensing their auras first. This requires paying attention to how you feel in people's presence. Usually, sensing is easier when that person isn't aware that you are trying to sense their aura. To sense a person's aura, you need to take a deep breath and exhale. Then, you need to focus on the physical sensations you are getting in your guts and body. What is your gut reaction? Focus on how being around that person makes you feel. What color would you attach to that person? As you work on enhancing your abilities, sensing and seeing people's auras will become easier than you can imagine.

As you practice these techniques to see human auras, you will find you blink while trying to focus, which makes the aura disappear. This is normal. If you relax your gaze and maintain your focus, the aura will quickly reappear in your vision. So, don't be afraid to blink, but don't let yourself blink too rapidly. If you blink rapidly than usual, it will become more challenging to get the aura to reappear in your vision.

When you see color in human auras, you may first see a single color. With time, you will see various colors in different parts of the aura. Some people believe that their eyes are deceiving them when this happens. This is not so. Remember than the auras can comprise different colors at a time. This is depending on whatever is happening within that person. The thoughts they have and the emotions they are experiencing. Also, don't forget that the brightness or dimness of a person's aura depends on how they feel. If the person whose aura you are looking at is happy and bubbly, their aura will be healthier, brighter, and bigger. When it is the opposite, their aura will look shrunk, weaker, and dimmer. A great way to see a person's aura in its glory when trying to read is to play their favorite music. This will strengthen their aura and make it bigger, clearer, and easier to see.

Reiterating, anyone can see auras if they put in the effort. Seeing human auras is all about consistency, patience, and practice.

Chapter Six: Auras of Plants and Animals

Like humans, plants and animals also have their own auras. This has been confirmed through science. First, I will talk about auras in plants and then about auras in animals. This will help you understand auras from their individual perspectives.

Everyone spiritually-inclined person who works with plants knows that they have their own auras. Some people have dedicated their time to studying plants' energetic properties. Unfortunately, most plants on earth nowadays don't have those energy qualities anymore. This is due to some reasons, including the pollution of the earth. Remember that the earth, just like the sun, is also a source of energy. And since plants grow directly from the earth, their energy is connected with that of the earth.

Another reason plants have lost their energy qualities throughout history is due to human ignorance. Unfortunately, several people don't believe in auras. Some people don't even believe *humans* have auras, much less *plants or animals!* As a result, they mess around with certain plants and use them for their own materialistic reasons. When you take care of plants well, you are improving the quality of their energy properties. Individuals who have worked on sharpening and developing their spiritual senses can usually see these properties in the surrounding plants.

Every plant energetically connects to the earth. This connection is established and maintained through the roots of these plants. They also energetically connect to the universe or cosmos and this connection is established through their leaves, flowers, and fruits. An inner energy channel runs through plants' stems, which connects the earth and cosmos energy with one another, including the plants. Plants also have an energy field that surrounds them, extending for about a few meters away. The energy field is the aura, and it is usually close to plants. The aura of plants is meant to be a protection, something to keep them healthy. The energy field is more assertive when a plant is healthy.

Through the aura, plants connect to their environment. This allows them to share and receive energy from other matters, objects, and beings in the same environment as them. This means that plants can communicate with other objects with auras. You can communicate with the plants in your garden through their auras if you want to. The aura of plants also connects to plants of the same species around the cosmos.

To See a Plant's Aura

Find a treasured plant in your garden. You could choose your favorite flower to practice it. To read this plant's aura, you will need your fingertip. But before you begin, seek permission from the plant. Gently ask if you can read its aura. Do not proceed until the plant has given you its response. If you don't "hear" or "feel" a yes, do not practice with that plant. A "yes" from the plant will typically feel like an inviting sensation, something warm and telling you to go ahead. If you aren't sure about how you can discern if a plant is permitting you to see its aura or not, you can experiment with different plants in your garden to find one that agrees. Gently use your fingertip to feel their energy. By experimenting, you will discern a "yes" and "no" from different non-human beings with aura. The plant's answer may be represented by a feeling, vision, a sense of clarity, a sense of smell, or a tingle. You can tell whether it is yes or no when you experience these sensations. If you don't feel like a plant is inviting you, this means that plant isn't permitting you to see its aura. Once you find a plant that says "yes" to having its aura observed and/or read, you can go ahead.

You will need to set your intention firmly. This means you will set your mind on admiring the aura of the plant that chooses you. You can set a timer for about 5 minutes. Do the exercise to charge yourself up and relaxed for the experience.

- Gently close your eyes and tune in with the plant. Move your fingertip around the plant gently. Do not touch the plant. Instead, touch the electricity in the air around the plant.

- Pay attention to the frequency you are receiving from the plant. How does it feel? You should receive specific colors and images, depending on the plant you are working with. Focus on the sensations you are receiving. Can you hear anything? Continue moving your fingertip around the plant until the 5 minutes on the timer is up.

- Once you are done, gently ask the plant if you can do anything to help. Do not take your fingertip away, so you hear or feel whatever the plant is saying.

It is vital to establish a "right" relationship with your plant (or animal) when connecting with their auric field. A right relationship is one where there are mutual respect and equal energy exchange between two objects or beings. You can have the right relationship between you and a loved one, your favorite flower, or you and your pet, cat, or dog.

Ensure you take enough time to listen to what the plant is saying. The plant may tell you whatever light or water requirements it has or anything else you need to know about it. When you have listened to the plant's needs, gently bow to it. After the aura-reading session with your plant, disentangle your own energy from the plant. Do this by gently rubbing your hands with each other; then, say, "I release the plant's energy back to it, whole and intact. I recall my energy back to myself, whole and intact." Feel as your energy returns to you, and the plant's energy returns to its root.

Animal Auras

Animals are animate objects; their energy is relatively easy to see. If you practice hard enough, you can start seeing the auras of inanimate objects such as your bed, table, book, or chair. Everything around you has an aura. If you have a cat, dog, or any other pet, know that animals also have an aura you can use to communicate with it. Animals have a vital role in the cosmos' grand plan. Yet, humans think of animals as things that exist to serve their own needs, neglecting that animals do have their own souls. Just like humans, animals are on an evolutionary path.

All animals look up to humans for love and inspiration. It is your duty as a human to help any animal around you in their spiritual development journey. Whether you have realized it or yet to, animals seek spiritual development like you. Evolution happens at every stage of life. Just as higher beings such as angels, archangels, and spirit guides help humans evolve, humans must help animals. Domestication is one way that you can help animals in this journey. When you take in a dog, cat, or any other animal as a pet, it shouldn't be solely to help yourself. See it as an opportunity to help that animal develop spiritually. Think of animals as spirit and energy sponges – they absorb the vibrational frequency they receive from you. So, when you radiate love, your pet absorbs that love from you. If you own a backyard farm or something similar, you have an excellent opportunity to help many animals. To help them in their spiritual development, you need to communicate and connect with their auras. This brings me back to the auras of animals.

Animals' auras are not as large and complex as humans. Yet, their auras are strong. Cats, for instance, have auras that extend about a foot from their body. Dogs have auras larger than cats. Auras in horses are even bigger than it is in cats and dogs. This shows that the size of the aura may vary from animal to animal. Like humans, animals' auras also change colors and sizes based on their feelings and moods. This is because they experience joy, sadness, fear, and anger, just as humans do. Also, animals are psychic by nature. They are like little children. They see the spiritual energies around themselves and the surrounding humans. Animals can reach a stage where they can tune in with the higher being inside of them. Through this, they also go through enlightenment and assume qualities primarily identified with humans. In more ways than one, animals are sometimes in tune with the spiritual more than most humans. This happens until humans learn to awaken the higher being inside of them.

You have likely heard of a pet whisperer before. These are people that can communicate with animals and convince them to do certain things. Pet whisperers can do this by communicating and reading the auras of their subject. Animal auras tell them everything they need to know about their needs and feelings. If you own pet (s), you should be able to sense, feel, and communicate with your pet through its aura. This is why it is helpful to also learn about plants and animals' auras. To be an aura reader, you must read the auras of animate and inanimate objects.

Pets have less complicated auras than humans because their emotions, thoughts, feelings, and moods are not as multifaceted as those of humans. When you try to sense and read your pet's aura, don't be surprised if it doesn't have more than one or two colors that blend into each other. In the ancient world, animals such as cats were recognized for their mystical qualities. Some people worshipped them for it, while some feared them. Regardless, it is a consensus throughout history that cats are occult creatures. A prevalent belief among many people, spiritual or not, is that cats can see ethereal bodies faster and sooner than other animals, including dogs with their keen senses. Naturally, when dogs see a spiritual being, they either ignore or bark/howl at it – depending on whether it is an evil spirit or a good one.

But cats react as they would were they looking at an actual human. A cat will watch a spirit as vividly and intensely as if it were looking at a human. If the spirit is harmless, the cat may be restless without getting aggressive and angry. A malevolent spirit would make the cat act aggressively. For example, it might spit at the invisible being. Many people keep cats as pets just to use them as a compass for knowing when a malevolent spirit is around.

Back to your pet's aura, it is relatively easy to tune in with your pet's aura. When you see your pet striding or bouncing towards you, just focus your eyes above the pet (peripherally) and try to sense its energy as it comes closer. This method is simple and straightforward. It also works best when the pet is off-focus, and you have tuned in with your own energy. So, consider trying this when you have just returned home, and your pet is in the mood to welcome you. Pets are always happier than usual, which means their aura will be more expanded and more comfortable to see. But with time, you can see your pet's aura, whether it is happy or otherwise.

After a few months of practice, you can identify the colors in your pet's aura. I should note that there's no definitive number of colors that an animal's aura may have. But they tend to not have more than one or two colors because I stated earlier. There would be an overall color you will come to identify in your pet's aura. This will be the primary color. It could be anything from yellow to beige to apricot. But there will also be a secondary, complementary color that blends with the primary color yet remains separable. When your pet is in a great mood, its aura will shine brightly and take on a striking look; almost like it will explode. When it isn't feeling so good, the color (s) will mix with black or gray, causing the aura to become dim, cloudy, and opaque. If you check your pet's aura and you find little cloudy holes, it means that your pet isn't healthy. If the holes are black, this portrays something even more sinister, like an accident.

You can talk to animals through their aura. Learning to do this, like everything else in this chapter, requires constant practice. However, it isn't as hard as when you are practicing seeing human auras. First, you need to become comfortable sensing your pet's aura and feeling its energy. This should be easy if you are a spiritually-inclined person. Allow your pet's aura to blend with your own energy field often. You shouldn't repel your dog's energy, as this can make the pet feel unwanted and unhappy. When trying to communicate with your pet's aura, start by caressing. While caressing your pet, make sure you are "saying" what you want to communicate with the animal. Focus on that thought and allow it to reverberate through your energy field to that of your pet. By doing this, you are conveying the message from your mind into its own. Your thought will become your pet's. Continue this for some time, and soon, you will find you can communicate with your pet through its aura. Not only will you be able to communicate with your pet, but the animal can also communicate with you. In short, you will be able to understand its thoughts because it will come to share them with you. This precisely is how pet whisperers communicate with animals.

Before I end this chapter, I want to go back briefly to cats and auras. I'm focusing on cats because they are more spiritually-inclined than dogs or most animals generally. Cats can sense and alter negative energy wherever they are. This is why many people say that their cats evoke a sense of peace and tranquil in their homes. Ask any cat owner you meet, and they will likely confirm this to you. The inner tranquil from living with a cat is much deeper than what you feel when your dog welcomes you back from work happily. This is linked to cats' abilities to sense and correct negative energy. Some healers who are also cat owners have talked about how their cats complement their energies, making it easier to heal humans and other animals. So, when trying to heal your auras or chakras and feel like your energy isn't enough, cuddling with your cat can amplify your energy. Cats can sense when the energy and aura of a person are negative or blocked. And they can also correct the negativity and unblock whatever is blocked by doing healing therapy. Most healers and psychics believe that having cats in their houses makes the energy more balanced and grounded.

Animals have auras; they also serve a higher purpose in ways that ordinary humans don't pay attention to or bother about. They mostly do this by giving themselves out to help humans. This is why cats and dogs are substantial support systems for humans. It is all part of nature, and, as a human, do everything you can to establish the right relationship with your household pets. As they help you, also help them. Regularly check their auras and see if they need you to help them with anything. You can use your own energies to help an animal that needs healing; so, never hesitate to do that when the situation arises. Remember that animals are also spiritually powerful. So, when you tune in with their auras to glean information, you may find a couple of things that may be very helpful for you. By allowing and doing this, you are playing your role in fulfilling the cosmos' divine plan.

Remember that this also applies to plants. Plants also play a role in the cosmic plan. Be as gentle as possible with them. Seek wisdom from them and let them be your guide in cases where you seem lost. You'd be surprised at just how helpful animals and plants can be when you regularly communicate and interact with their energy fields.

Now that you know how to perceive, sense, feel, and see auras in humans, plants, animals, and even inanimate objects, how do you interpret what you see when observing people's auras. This is precisely what the next chapter covers. Read on!

Chapter Seven: Aura Colors and Their Meanings

Aura colors are the key to aura reading. If you can sense or see the aura without knowing how to understand what you see, you are not really an aura reader. Reading the aura is all about learning how to see the aura; more important, learning the interpretation of what you see. When you see specific colors in a person's aura or your own, what does it mean for that person? What do the colors in color represent? What do they stand for? How do you use the colors to predict things about a person? These and more are what this chapter hopes to help you understand.

Before I delve into the complexities of aura colors, there are basic things you should know about colors in the auric layers. An individual's aura color represents their personality, relationship dynamics, and professional inclination. Knowing the colors of a person's aura gives you insight into helping them understand themselves. But that is not all. It also helps you help them be who they are supposed to be. For instance, reading and interpreting a person's aura colors can tell you about that job they are stuck in and how they can get out of it. The aura can even help people learn financial freedom and independence. There are so many things that are understandable simply through an understanding of aura colors.

There is no definitive way to answer, "what do the colors of the aura mean?" Colors have different meanings, depending on several factors. Meanings of auric colors are affected by the vibrations in the auric field a person's body language, the part of the body you are watching or observing, and the environmental or circumstantial effects of the surroundings on the person whose aura is being observed. As a rule of thumb, an aura reader should never base their judgment on the colors that appear in a layer of the aura. These colors tend to go through changes, depending on what they mean. For example, you can look at someone at this moment and see a specific color in one of their auric layers. Take your eyes away for a few minutes, return it to them, and you might find that the color has changed to a new one. You can't base your readings solely on that one color you initially saw. Even when you know the meanings of aura colors, consider other factors when observing and reading a person's aura.

It's quite common for people who only started learning how to see and read auras to see pale colors before becoming more apparent and more vivid. When you are at that point in progress, note that pale colors rarely have any relevance to understanding the subtle energy bodies and people as a whole. Suppose you get to where you can see brighter and more precise colors while some parts of the aura remain weak. There, the person is experiencing weakness in any aspect of their personal, professional, or spiritual life. You need to consider many things to identify the cause of that weakness. It could be physical, mental, emotional, or spiritual. Soon, I will share more information on the general guidelines for interpreting the colors in an aura.

In pop culture, it is a common misconception that aura colors have a straightforward meaning. Some people believe that yellow means optimism; red means passion; purple means spirituality, and so on like that. This is a tactic of oversimplifying the power of the auric field. The aura doesn't stick to a color code. Red in one layer can mean something today and mean another thing tomorrow. Aura colors will vary from person to person due to the variations of colors available in the aura. There are tons of hues, shades, and tones within each color in the aura that could all mean different things. Each shade of one specific color in the aura communicates different meanings to the person who is reading.

As an example: Let's talk about the color blue. A light shade of blue portrays something different from a darker shade of blue. This is due to the slight differences in shade and tone. Each of the tones in one color expresses different meanings about the aura. This is why it is crucial to learn the colors' meanings and how to interpret them according to their unique shades. This can be compared to when a person is picking paint colors for their new house. You must go through tons of color swatches to get the right tone of paint you want for your house. There will be so many subtle variations of colors; some you will like and some you won't. It won't matter if they are all tones within the same color. Each tone will give you a different feeling. This is the same thing that happens with aura colors. Different tones of one aura color can communicate different feelings and meanings to an aura reader. So, it doesn't help to fixate on one definitive meaning stamped by pop culture.

Remember that the colors of a person's aura can be affected by the vibrations and energies of people around them. The colors in your aura can change depending on who you are with at a particular time. It's common for people to get other people's auric colors in their own aura, especially when their energies interconnect. Something like this happens where you claim that "I can just feel myself connect to this person." Sometimes, parents put a color from their own aura into their child's own just because they want the child to behave in a way they also behave. This is a deceptive practice and shouldn't be encouraged. In cases like this, the affected person might struggle with inner unrest, confusion, a loss of the self, and other health issues. This means that doing this can cause a lot of problems for your children. So, it is not something you are encouraged to do.

Fortunately, a good thing about the aura is there are general color themes that can guide you to interpret the meaning. Note that the meanings of aura colors depend on the shades, tone, and the person whose aura you are observing or reading.

Red

Red is the color associated with the root chakra, which is the base chakra noted in an earlier part of the book. This color stands for physical energy, passion, determination, change, power, survival, courage, and action. It is a color found in the aura of people who love to take charge of their lives themselves. People who have red in their auras tend to be those with an understanding of physical realities. They relish manifesting their desires in the physical realm. They do everything with passion and are unafraid to embrace their daring and adventurous nature. This makes them unapologetic about experiencing life as it comes. This passion and courage make them very driven and oriented. They are not afraid of mortality, birth, sensuality, and indulgence. They sometimes enjoy over-indulgence. When someone emits red in their aura, it means they are the kind of person that does not deny themselves the many pleasures of life.

This color can either appear bright and radiant or weak and dark in people. A slight change in the brightness or saturation of the color red can mean so many things. If the red appears like scarlet or ruby, it points to vibrancy, vitality, ability to tackle and overcome challenges, and an inherent desire to engineer positive change in the world. It may also indicate being a passionate lover. But a darker shade of red indicates frustration, anger, or trauma. It may also point to the person being a bully and impulsive. It may also represent exhaustion, low vibrational frequency, and a state of being overworked. Flashing red suggests a flirty and inappropriately passionate nature.

Be as discerning of this color's many shades when you find it in a person's aura. This will help you avoid misinterpretation of what you see.

Orange

Orange is the color typically associated with the sacral chakra. And as you have learned, this chakra is tied with sensuality and creativity. It is also directly connected with the emotional layer of the auric field. This suggests that it has a lot to do with emotions. Orange represents the center for relationships, friendships, and interactions. Individuals with this color in their auras value their relationships, whether personal or professional. Also, lively exchange in terms of money, time, resources, energy, work, or love makes them radiate and resonate better with others.

Due to their ability to seamlessly establish mutually-respective relationships with others, people with orange aura color are good with teamwork. They are highly sociable and relatable. They can also be perceptive and dynamic. They embrace change and will let it happen. If you meet a person with an orange aura, you are unlikely to remain a stranger for long. They simply have a knack for developing friendships quickly. They are relationship experts. A person who has orange in their aura will find it challenging to stay still because they want to experience the world. You can call them thrill-seekers because one thing they will never do is sit around and wait for adventures to seek them out. Because they crave newness, freshness, and sensation, they can either become addicted to relationships or cannot stay committed in their relationships. This depends on the frequency the color orange is vibrating at.

When the color orange is warm and rich in a person's aura, it indicates an ability to effortlessly integrate several aspects of their lives: sociability, relatability, originality, creativity, and self-motivation. It also indicates a free-thinking, enthusiastic, open-minded, and optimistic nature. Bright and radiant orange is an excellent color to find in anyone trying to have children. Paler orange suggests low self-esteem or a loss of identity. When someone has a paler shade of orange in their aura, it may mean they are out of tune with their true self. This makes them live their life based on the opinions and thoughts of other people. Such a person may be susceptible to bullying. Sometimes, orange may also appear murky in a person's aura. When this happens, it means that person may be overly sensitive, egoistic, possessive, and likely territorial. Harsh orange indicates an obsession with self-image.

Yellow

Yellow, as you can probably tell, is the color of the sunny and cheery people. It is the color of the solar plexus chakra. This chakra is linked with self-esteem, intellect, and personal power. Yellow is associated with mental dexterity, versatility, intellectual accomplishments, controversial abilities, restlessness, and a sense of changeability. Individuals who emit yellow in their energy field are full of confidence in their abilities. They typically have a strong sense of self, meaning they are in tune with whom they really are. They resonate with happiness, powerful self-esteem, and the natural ability to inspire people to desire and seek greatness. Yellow-aura people are born leaders. They have an incredibly high level of energy, which makes them able to positively motivate the people around them.

People who have yellow emissions in their auras also positively support and encourage others without losing a sense of whom they are. They are like the sun – radiating and shining their light on others. They also can analyze and break down concepts that appear complex to other people. Individuals with yellow auras are full of inner happiness and joy, making them radiate warmly like the sun. You can always feel a sense of warmth when you are around someone like that.

If the yellow in a person's aura is bright and clear as lemon, it shows someone with a focused mind and sharp memory. Such a person will also have strong business acumen, meaning they will be excellent at handling finances and other related concepts. Bright yellow also communicates joy and openness. It may also suggest someone who will make a great entertainer or actor. If the bright yellow has a brown hint, it augurs an individual with a mathematical or scientific mind.

Harsh streaks in the color yellow can be a sign of hyperactivity. Mustard yellow points to resentment and jealousy. A shade of metallic yellow indicates a dishonest intent and a proclivity towards gambling and shady activities—a sharp tone of yellow points to someone logical and highly sarcastic. A cold shade of yellow indicates someone who puts their head over their heart more often than not. If you observe a darker and denser yellow shade, it suggests overconfidence, perfectionism, and self-criticism. It could also mean that a person is operating from the ego-driven self.

Green

Green is the heart chakra; its color resonates with it as the place for growth and healing. People with the color green in their aura emit unconditional love. Their life force is so powerful and robust that it is instantly perceived by all beings that are in their presence, human or not. Due to this, green-aura individuals are drawn to nature, and animals. They do have natural healing abilities. When you are in the presence of someone who emits green from their aura, you may feel a sense of peace and calm you won't feel with anybody else. They are some of the most grounded people when it comes to auric colors. They can equally share their attention between their loved ones and their creative ambitions. For example, if a father emits green in his auric field, he's more likely to be a devout father to his children no matter how busy he gets chasing his own goals. Green-aura individuals possess a great sense of responsibility and service, particularly to the people around them. They are incredibly self-assertive. The green aura is the bridge between the physical and spiritual planes. Thus, people with green auras are typically focused on people with great ideals and lofty aspirations. They are also profoundly creative.

A clear and rich green tone indicates a loving and trustworthy individual generous with their love, money, and time. It also indicates someone who expresses themselves from their heart. A green aura can indicate a person committed to the people they love. In the emerald shade, green shows a person with natural healing abilities, particularly in the alternative healing field. It also points to a person with natural luck. When green turns place, it may suggest emotional codependency. Dully, muddy green points to conflicting emotions inside or an energy vampire, someone who sucks other people's energy. Green, with a hint of yellow, reveals traits such as possessiveness and emotional unavailability. Lime green implies stressful relationships. Dark green in the aura indicates unrequited love or unequal love.

Blue

Blue is the color associated with the throat chakra, which is the center of self-expression and communication. A person with blue in their aura has the natural ability to express themselves and speak their truths. They are naturally expressive, so they can also give naturally expressive and thoughtful gifts to loved ones for birthdays and anniversaries. Those with blue in their aura possess inner wisdom and knowledge. Their feelings are all they need to figure out what is right or wrong; they don't need data or facts to know things. Due to their expressiveness, they value personal relationships greatly. They desire clarity and honesty in their relationships, but not just from their partners; they work on achieving mutual trust and responsibility. Blue-aura people love sharing wisdom and gathering wisdom from others. They make exceptional philosophers.

A shade of royal blue in the aura suggests an integrated personality and someone with natural leadership abilities and a sharp sense of justice. Brighter blue indicates altruism and creativity. Pale blue suggests an idealist with a tremendous global vision. Clearer blue stands for objectivity; an individual with clear blue in their aura may be a teacher or gifted public speaker. You may find the color blue suffusing other auric colors in healers, authors, musicians, and other people in the entertainment field. A dull shade of blue represents conservatism and rigidity. Such people keep to the rules, despite circumstances. Harsh blue may suggest an autocratic individual who is highly opinionated. Such a person may also be intolerant of the lifestyle and beliefs of others.

Generally, though, the lighter the tone of blue in a person's aura, the more positive and peaceful the energy they radiate will be. So, when you are in the presence of someone, and you feel an incredible calm, their aura may be blue in color.

Indigo

Indigo is the third-eye chakra's color. It relates to a keen sense of knowing and intuition. In the color spectrum, indigo has the second-highest vibrational frequency. Anybody with indigo in their aura possesses powerful, intuitive gifts that may not be conscious of yet. They are always in tune, which makes them super sensitive to the energy radiating from others. They have a knack for knowing things before they even happen. They can also have lucid and literal dreams. Their sensitivity to others' energy makes them empathetic. They are what we call highly sensitive people.

People with indigo on their auras operate from a place of feeling vs. logic. They are naturally seekers, and they understand that the world is bigger than the individuals in it. They also understand the importance of going with the flow of life and living the moment. Indigo-aura people believe in their intuition, plus they can naturally tell the truth from illusion. As they are mostly communicators, they can help other people understand the cosmos' vast beauty and its many mysteries.

A bright indigo color suggests sensitivity to unspoken intentions and an in-depth awareness of the spiritual realm. It also points to clairvoyance, intuition, and clairaudience. Clearer shades of indigo represent a fertile and active imagination. Deeper shades are found in the auras of older, wise people. Indigo, with a hint of lavender, suggests the acknowledgment of the higher powers present within nature. People with this possess a gift for herbalism.

On the other hand, blurred indigo shades imply obsession with illusions and daydreams. It also means that the person may be soaking up negative energies from other people—dark shades of indigo points to disillusionment and isolation from the world. A hazy shade of indigo represents a disconnect from intuition and self-doubt.

Violet

This is the color of the crown chakra. The crown chakra is connected with your higher consciousness. People with violet emissions in their auras have compelling personalities; they are charismatic and dynamic. They believe that their mission in life is to help, lead, and inspire others. Their task is to inspire the world into an age of prosperity. Violet-aura people have a drive and inner urge to achieve important things with their life. They believe in having a higher purpose, and they do their best to live up to it. They are also visionaries with great ideals and hopes for the future of humanity. Thanks to their knowledge and gift of intuition, they can see the bigger picture usually without being overwhelmed by the details. They are naturally sensitive people, which makes it easy for them to empathize with others.

Individuals with violet auras desire an intimate connection with the universe and everything within it. They are like an open book to all. Their vibration frequency is relatively high, which makes them connected with other invisible forms of life force energy. Those with violet in their energy field can manifest their projections into the physical world. There is a great deal of originality in their thoughts, ideas, and insights. And no matter what, they always show a high level of concern for the universe and life matrix.

In its bright and vibrant shade, violet represents deep wisdom and collective knowledge of humanity. It also indicates an ability to take the globe into perspective when thinking, which makes violet-aura people disregard material gain as the primary purpose of achieving their goals. However, a paler shade of violet signifies a lack of drive and incentive. It may also mean that one's grand plan rarely become accomplished. Harsh violet portrays a need for perfectionism, and unrealistic expectations and goals. A person with harsher shades of violet in their aura may not handle imperfections, whether it is theirs or others. Dull violet is an indication of depression.

White

When one has transcended the material realm's obstacles and limitations, their aura turns a pure, all-white color with no other color present. This color is rare in people's auras. Only a handful of people in the physical realm have white as their auric color. And these people are usually those who have freed themselves from the issues and challenges of life. The most common you will see is people with white and other colors in their aura. An all-white aura is rare. People with an all-white aura have successfully reached a state where they are always spiritually motivated and remain open and receptive to the cosmos and its energy. Such people have no concern with worldly ambitions and matters. They are all about purity and honesty. A white aura means you are operating from a place of positivity, upliftment, and non-judgment.

Vibrant white is found in people who follow their unique life path without questions. Such people can make their mark on the world. Pale and misty white may show someone seeking answers to specific questions they have about the universe.

Magenta

Individuals with magenta in their aura are the definition of originality. Magenta is a mix of blue and red frequencies in the energy field. It's usually between those two in the color spectrum. People who emit magenta in their aura have mastered an understanding of the physical world while possessing an enhanced capacity for thinking intuitively. This makes them the ideal candidates for creative work. They are naturally creative people with a high energy frequency. Thus, they thrive on being original and innovative. They don't enjoy being copycats. Because of their need to experience the world in their own way, they may appear eccentric to other people. But people are generally positively receptive to them. Magenta-aura people don't allow peer pressure to influence them. They are strong-willed and optimistic. They also have a great sense of humor.

Rich magenta is typically found in spiritual leaders. It is considered the aura of wise people who have acquired wisdom through experience. More important, they also use that experience to benefit others. But the color can also be found in younger people, particularly those who refuse to let challenges defeat them. Harsh magenta is found in false spiritual leaders, especially those trying to use their powers to dominate people. It is also characteristic of spiritual leaders with inflated knowledge.

Pink

This is one of the rarest colors to appear in an aura. A baby pink aura is found in people with a gentle nature and a loving nature that radiates pleasantly towards everyone around them. People with pink auras are sensitive, romantic, and relatable. They can keep the flames of their relationships going due to their penchant for romantic gestures. They are also creative, with healing and intuition. Pink vibrates at the same frequency as the color green, which is connected with the heart chakra.

People who emit pink in their aura are bubbly and uplifting. They inspire feelings of comfort in those around them. Even in the face of challenges, a person with a pink aura keeps uplifting others with smiles and kind words. They are gentle with all the earth's creatures.

Chapter Eight: Cleansing and Healing the Aura

Tell me if this sounds familiar. You feel sick, irritated, and wound up. It's starting to become too often. You can't bring yourself to get enough sleep as you should, and you feel like your mind and body are in a constant state of exhaustion. You have no idea what to do. When you start to feel like this, it is a sign that the time to clean and heal your aura has come. Unless you do this, you might come down with a significant illness.

Your aura is your protective shell that always surrounds you. The aura is heavily affected by the people you interact with and the situations you get into. Every day of your life, you are continually exchanging energies with people you come across or interact with. This dramatically affects your auric field. As a result, the aura gets weak from the clutters of energy debris from those around you. You may even soak up the negative energy and emotions of people like a sponge. Eventually, you start to feel stressed, irritable, anxious, lethargic, and impatient. You may even develop an unpleasant outlook on life. Your immune system might become weaker, leaving vulnerable to sickness and diseases. Fortunately, it is easy to cleanse your aura from the comfort of your home. You just need a little practice to get started. Once you learn how to cleanse your aura and heal it., there will be a significant difference in your mental and physical health. In short, your mind and body will be in a calm and peaceful state.

There are several ways you can cleanse and heal your aura. When looking for a reasonable alternative medicine practice to help with your condition, it is okay to be picky. This is why different techniques exist to help different people. The good thing about aura cleansing is that it always improves one's quality of life, including other things such as happiness and joy. It also reduces the symptoms of stress and anxiety. One by one, let's discuss four different energy healing techniques that are very effective for cleansing and healing the aura.

Smudging

Smudging is the ritual of sage burning. This ritual can get rid of the negative energy from oneself and one's environment. Sage, which is the essential ingredient in smudging, is a plant from the Salvia family. The word "Salvia" is derived from Salvere, a Latin word which means "To heal." Besides sage's spiritual use, scientific research has shown that it has physical, mental, and emotional benefits. Spiritually, it is generally believed that smudging keeps harmful and toxic energy away. Think of smudging as a way of clearing your aura so more positivity can enter the energy centers.

As a beginner to the practice of smudging, you will need a few essential items to do it. You can easily find a sage kit on the internet. But if there is a metaphysical shop in your local area, you can check there too. If you are sensitive to smoke, there are cleansing smudge mists to help you. Basically, you will need sage, a vessel (for burning sage), a candle or long match, and an optional fanning tool. Once you have the tools, you can get started with smudging your aura.

- Set your intention for smudging. This is to clarify that you are trying to purify and release harmful elements from your aura. You will also need to choose a mantra you will repeat as you go through the process of smudging. Thankfully, you can come up with a mantra on your own. Example: "I command any low vibrational energy, negativity, and toxicity within my aura to leave and go into the light. You are not wanted. Leave and go into the light."

- Once you are ready to begin, light the sage with your candle or long match, hold it away at a 45-degree angle, and leave it to burn for at least 20 seconds. After this, blow out the flame and watch the smoke billow up.

- Stand in a T shape with your legs spread apart a little. Then, start from your feet and work your way up. As you move the sage stick around your body, keep repeating your mantra, internally or aloud. Visualize the negativity being released from your body into the smoke of the sage stick.

That's it! However, be sure to determine the areas of your aura that need the smudging more. Be careful not to inhale the smoke of the sage; keep it at arm's length as you work. Also, remain grounded as you work your way from your feet upwards. Once you are done, don't forget to extinguish the sage stick. There is no definite schedule for smudging, but it is something you should regularly do if you want your aura to stay clean and powerful. Do it whenever you feel stress, or are anxious and irritable.

Crystals

Crystals are incredibly useful tools for cleansing the aura and improving one's spiritual wellbeing. They are also powerful. Crystals emit energy, which is why they can also clear it when you need them to. They have a positive calming and neutralizing effect on people. Different types of crystals may be used for aura cleansing. However, some are just more effective than others. Each type of crystal cleanses the aura in its own unique way. Understand the cleansing properties of a crystal before you use it. Below are powerful crystals for cleaning your aura.

- **Celestite:** Celestine is a powerful purifying crystal that brings instant calm and harmony to the mind. Celestite refreshes your mind and uplifts your mood. And it can help you in periods of transition and changes. Carrying this crystal with you can help get rid of negative thoughts and overwhelming feelings. It attunes you with the spiritual realm.

- **Amethyst Spirit Quartz:** Using amethyst crystal is like having an auric bath of brilliant, sparkling lights. This crystal detoxifies your aura, whole rejuvenating your mind and body. It is safe to call amethyst spirit quartz the soul's spa treatment because it does treat the soul. It is excellent for detoxifying your emotions and body, particularly from the spirit of addiction. Always keep this crystal with you to ward off negative energy from your aura.

- **Aqua Aura:** From the name, you can already tell this is an unmistakable aura treatment crystal. Aqua aura possesses a strong cleansing vibration, making it great to clear, balance, and align your chakras. Once the chakras are cleaned, balanced, and aligned, the aura automatically becomes purified. This crystal is useful for releasing stuck energy and toxic debris. You can also use it to infuse yourself with inspiration whenever you feel stuck in one position.

- **Herkimer Diamond:** The final crystal I recommend for aura cleansing is the Herkimer diamond. It is a deep cleanser whose vibrations can penetrate the physical layer to deeply cleanse any negative energy or elements from the aura. It cleanses the mind. Herkimer diamond helps eliminate incoherent and discordant thoughts, after which it replaces them with harmonizing ones. It can also block your aura from picking up the negative energies and emotions of others. This can be helpful for empaths and highly sensitive people. The properties in the diamond help establish clear and vibrant vibrations in the energy field.

Crystals are super useful for cleansing the aura and healing them of toxicity.

Aura Bathing

Having an aura cleansing bath is one of the best ways to get your aura to literally shine and sparkle. An aura bath can revive and rejuvenate the aura so it is soothing and restorative to your mind and body. It is easy to have an aura cleansing bath, but you will need a couple of items to get it done. You will need a bathtub, but that is not all. You will also need sea salt, essential oils, and a journal (optional). Some of the best sea salts and essential oils I recommend include Himalayan sea salt, Dead sea salt, Hawaiian sea salt, and Lavender essential oil. Once you have the required items, you can bathe.

Before you bathe, ensure that you have some alone time where nothing will disturb you, not even your phone. Consider putting it on "Do Not Disturb." Also, you shouldn't forget to set your intention. Although easy, you can't just hop into the bathtub and start bathing. The intention is fundamental when you are having any spiritual bath. Set your intention regarding what you want to do – restore and refresh your aura. Next, fill in your tub with lukewarm water. Don't use utterly cold water; it should at least be a little warm. Then, add in the lavender essential oil. The refreshing scent will prove super relaxing for the bath. If you use Himalaya sea salt, mix it in with the water before going in the water. Otherwise, wait until you are in the water and then use it as a scrub for your skin.

Now, enter the bathtub and get to visualizing. Visualization is a powerful technique for cleansing your aura. Mix water and sea salt together and scrub your skin gently. Visualize yourself, scrubbing away the emotions and energy that your aura accumulated over time. If you aren't scrubbing, visualize yourself healing your aura of the negative energy it has soaked up recently. Imagine your aura returning to its vibrant and sparkling state. Then, visualize yourself surrounded by white light. Picture as the light swallows everything that is no longer of benefit to you and your aura. Once you are done, get rid of the water in your tub and put on some comfortable clothes. Consider relaxing with some herbal tea. You should feel relaxed, relieved, and free from stress.

Meditation and Visualization

Meditation is another effective aura cleansing technique you can try. Cleansing your aura with meditation requires you to possess chakra awareness, which essentially means knowing the seven chakra locations in your body. If you don't already know this, go back to the chapter where we discussed the seven chakra positions in the energy system and master chakra awareness. Then, you can do the chakra meditation to cleanse your aura.

- Start from the root chakra, which is also called the grounding chakra. It is at the base of the spine, and its color is red. Remembering this, visualize your root chakra having a flaming, red light extending from under it, serving as its anchor to the earth.

- Next, imagine yourself being engulfed in brilliant, golden light anchored to the sun. Imagine this light penetrating every part of your body and aura. Visualize it engulfing you for some minutes.

- Then, visualize a shower of violet light coming up from your soles to the top of your head. Feel it enclose you, serving as a warm and protective blanket. Know that the violet light will heal all holes within your aura and protect you. Imagine as the light closes the holes one by one, leaving your aura closed to negative energies. With this imagery in your head, you have started your cleansing and healing process.

- You should feel yourself becoming lighter and stronger. Your aura will start to release the negative and toxic energies, causing you to feel a sense of calm in your mind, body, and soul. You should also become more in tune with unseen divine energies. Meditate on the sensation you are feeling for some time. Then, visualize a white light appear around your aura.

You have successfully cleaned and healed your aura. You can enjoy the benefits of a cleansed, sparkling, and vibrant aura. Note that this particular meditation technique requires practice. Practice it as often as you need to make yourself comfortable using the healing lights.

Chapter Nine: Protecting the Aura

You must learn how to protect your energy field. The aura, as I have reiterated several times, can be likened to a sponge. It picks up, sometimes soak up, the energies of everybody around you. It doesn't matter whether the energies are positive or negative; your aura will pick it up and even accommodate it. So, you must learn how to protect your aura. This means shielding your aura to prevent it from absorbing negative and toxic energies or emotions. A strong aura equals a positive and healthy mind. Unless your aura is protected, your mind and body will be susceptible to attacks. After all, the aura is supposed to be the body's protective shield. Anything that affects the aura will eventually affect the body. This shows why illnesses and diseases begin in the auric field before they even manifest in the physical body.

A healthy mind is probably the most important thing an individual can possess. A healthy mind with a weak body can be managed; however, it would be difficult to handle a healthy body and a weak mind. A weak mind will make the body susceptible to all sorts of attacks, spiritual or otherwise. Protecting your aura entails understating your ability to protect your mind and your thoughts. Remember that the aura is an extension of you. Leaving it fragile and damaged can make you disconnected from your mind. This, in turn, may make you disconnected from reality.

Your intention matters. You need to set the intention of protecting your energy field because this is what really protects you. When you form a protective shield around your aura, you need to be convinced that it is really there. A firm conviction is vital, which is why the mind is so important. You need to be convinced that your protective shield is there, even if you cannot see it. You need to have a firm conviction that the shield is impenetrable, meaning unseen or seen negative energies will not infiltrate it. Be confident that it will do its job of protecting you. Being doubtful or showing signs of fear or uncertainty can weaken the protective shield and make it penetrable by unwanted energies. The great thing about a protective shield is that you can put it up around anyone you love, from your child to your partner. Remember that all things have their own aura. So, you can also put it around your home, car, and everything else you want to protect. Anybody or anything can benefit from this energy protection. As a matter of fact, everything needs energy protection. When repelling energy to create a protective shield around your aura, don't forget to do it with a positive mindset. Send the negative energies down to the Earth with love and light; this will help them heal. This is why it is vital to visualize a white light when sending negative energy away. Always trust your intuition and believe in your inner guidance.

So, how do you protect your aura from negative energies and emotions?

First, you can teach yourself to become nonreactive. This means learning to respond instead of reacting to volatile reactions. When someone is angry with you, the best way to protect your energy in that situation is to detach from the experience. You also need to stay as calm as possible. When you do this, your energy will remain unaffected by the negative emotional expression. Be clear about the situation so you can respond in a detached way. Avoid forming an attachment to the display of anger if you aren't in a dangerous situation. If you can, do your best to bring the person out of that state of anger. You can ask how you can help them or simply apologize for the situation. Or you can listen to them express themselves without interrupting. This can decrease the intensity of their emotions. Reacting instead of responding to anger makes you vulnerable to the negative energy threatening to explode from the person. The negativity may become attached to your auric field.

Instead of reacting, use your heart to bless that person so their anger may become calm. Concentrate on your heart chakra, and wish that their negative energy becomes that of peace, love, and understanding. This will make you feel better since you aren't depleting your energy by reacting to their anger. Doing this may be difficult, but don't take your mind away from love.

Second, always use love to protect yourself from negative energies. Doing this means remaining grounded in love. Love is a powerful and positive force that can repel negativity. Love empowers; the strength of a loving aura can keep any negative energy from infiltrating your aura. Negative energy can't attach to your aura if your thoughts and feelings don't welcome such energy. Love keeps you from radiating negative vibrations. Always think of love and light.

Third, you should always return negative energy back into Mother Earth. When you sense negative energy around you, take a deep breath, exhale, and ask the energy to leave your environment. Visualize yourself sending that energy into the Earth. Don't forget to do this with love, light, and healing. You can add a prayer when sending the energy back into the earth. Ask Mother Earth to bless the energy so it can regenerate into positive energy. If you don't want to send the energy into the Earth, you can cleanse it with fire yourself. Simply envision a bucket of fire and visualize yourself, putting the negative energy into the fire. Then, ask the Divine to recycle the energy into a positive one with love, light, and healing.

Another way to protect your aura from negative energy is to close the aura. It is easily one of the simplest things to do to protect your aura. You only need minutes to do it. It entails making your aura compact and dense, making it difficult to penetrate. Closing your aura requires you to be fully conscious of what you are doing. To close your aura, sit down in a meditative pose. Then, cross your legs and place your palms on your lower abdominal area. You can also cross your arms completely. You need not use visualization for this technique. Your intention is all you need to close the aura. You can easily use this technique when you are in a business meeting, an airport, or at a party. It blocks the people around you in these places from draining your energy. It is handy for protecting yourself from energy vampires. When you leave the public place and reach a safe space, you can reset your intention, opening up your aura to receive love and light from your new environment. Don't forget to set it so that love and light can go out from you towards others.

Cocooning is another technique for protecting your aura. It is powerful, and many people have testified to its effectiveness. Cocooning your body entails visualizing a ball of white and golden light in the shape of a cocoon and allowing it to encircle you. You need to imagine the light from your feet to the legs to your thighs, waist, stomach, heart, and throat until you reach the top of your head, and your whole back. The cocoon should cover your entire body. Set your intention to keep negative energies from penetrating the cocoon while you keep radiating love and light to people you meet and the environment you are in. Cocooning can be used whenever you are traveling, receiving guests in your home, or working. You can use it when walking the streets at night.

You can also use the Prana technique of sweeping negative energy from your aura. Just as you clean your home and rid it of clutter through sweeping, prana can clear your energy field of old and unwanted energy. You may also use it to eliminate thoughts and feelings that no longer serve any purpose in your life. Sweeping old energies away from your aura restores your connection with your energy field, and the Divine or Higher Being. This method can clear emotions such as pain, anger, fear, self-doubt, self-hatred, etc. Basically, you can sweep away any emotion that shouldn't be present in your life. When you do this, you are setting your consciousness from, so your mind, body, and soul can be free. The sweeping technique can be used quickly and swiftly. It is the ideal technique for you if you are the type that meets so many people every day. To sweep old energies from your aura:

- Cup your hands with each palm facing you. Let the fingers of your hands point towards one another, leaving about 3 feet distance between.

- Start 10 inches from your head, sweeping your hands downwards till you reach your feet.

- Set your intention and visualize the sweeping motion in the back of your body. Do this a few times until you get rid of all the negative energy.

Never sweep upward whenever you use this prana technique. Instead, ensure the sweeping motion always goes upward. Sweeping in a downward motion helps to clear the energy. Upwards sweeping can cause the congestion of energy. Remember to send the energies into the Earth as you sweep. You need not touch the physical body before this technique works to heal and balance your aura. It can positively affect your positive health. The more you use the technique, the lesser the chances of being affected by people's energies.

One exceptional technique I use for protecting my aura is the white bubble technique. You can use this technique anywhere, anytime, and as often as necessary to shield yourself from negative thoughts and energy. The white bubble technique will help you keep your mind in a continuous state of calm and peace.

- Visualize rays of white and golden lights fall on you from above. Make sure this light is of the purest and cleanest quality. It should pour from above onto your head, covering your whole being. You should feel as if you are engulfed in a bubble or something with a close and tight outline. Picture this light cleansing your being while forming a strong and impenetrable barrier.

As you visualize, repeat the white light prayer below to set your intention and make the bubble stronger.

I am surrounded by the light of the Divine

I am enfolded by the love of the Divine

I am protected by the power of the Divine

I am being watched by the presence of the Divine

The Divine is wherever I am, Amen

Note: You can replace "Divine" with whatever works best for you.

The white bubble technique may protect you from being penetrated by unwanted energy. Still, it doesn't stop positive energy from leaving or entering your aura. So, you can still send/receive love and light with other positive-energy people.

Protecting your aura is a vital part of your everyday activities. Use at least one of these techniques a few times every day. This is to keep you grounded and secure from unforeseen malicious energy attacks!

Chapter Ten: Daily Tips to Enhance Psychic Abilities

One can have latent psychic abilities without knowing how best to use them. I believe that everyone has psychic abilities that may be dormant. The abilities are merely there waiting for you to train and start exercising them. The more you train and use your psychic abilities, the more you astute you become. You need to exercise your psychic abilities just as you exercise the muscles and organs in your body. As a beginner, constant training is key to successfully learning how to work with the natural talents nature has bestowed on you. First, you must learn how to effectively quiet your mind and maintain a comfortable and harmonized mental state. This is key to facilitating focus on enhancing your abilities. Don't forget to regularly practice the techniques for quieting mental chatter, as discussed in an earlier chapter.

Psychic abilities should be hones just as you would hone all other skills. Just as you continuously train to learn a skill, keep this same energy for your aura reading and other psychic gifts. Below are exercises you can integrate into your routine easily. With daily practice of at least four of these techniques, you will become a professional psychic before you know it. Ensure you enjoy every step of the practice; it is crucial to learning.

- **Meditation:** Daily meditative sessions will help keep your mind and body in a relaxed and peaceful state, as they should be. Improving your psychic abilities requires a daily practice of the art of meditation. Clairvoyance, clairsentience, and other psychic abilities are all about attuning to your spirit. So, you need to learn to tune in with your center in little to no time. You need to do this with little effort. Consider starting with a focal point to concentrate on. A practical item to use for this practice is a scented candle. Focus on a candle's flame, and you will release yourself from all the chatter and noises in your head. Inhale and exhale naturally as you focus. Do not force or strain yourself. You can also do other forms of meditations, such as open-eyed meditation. This involves focusing on the clouds as they float by. Find out which works best for you.

- **Communicate with Your Spirit Guide:** When you go to the astral realm, you can meet and communicate with your spirit guide. Everyone has a spirit guide in the spirit world. The purpose of a spirit guide is to assist you in the life choices you make and the experiences you seek. They are always a thought away from you, even if you don't visit the astral realm. You can learn to connect with your spirit guide more consciously. When you do this, you have an opportunity to ask them to assist you in developing your psychic abilities. The more you communicate with your spirit guide, the easier it becomes to connect with them and seek spiritual guidance from them. There are much information and insight to gain from communicating with your guide; so, make this a habit!

- **Environmental Scans:** This is a method I regularly use to cultivate my psychic abilities. Basically, doing "environmental scans" is all about scanning your surroundings to determine the kind of energies around you and using your senses. To do an environmental scan, you need to sit in the center of your room. Then, move around the room with your eyes. As you do this, note the sounds, scents, and sights. Which parts of the rooms seem more inviting to your eyes? Which ones seem least inviting? Scan the windows, furniture, and corners. Note how the energy in these places makes you feel. It is okay to feel awkward the first time you try this exercise, but don't let the awkwardness deter you. No one will notice as you do your psychic explorations. You can practice this technique in your office, the park, a bar, and even subway transports. The whole point of environmental scans is to train you in becoming more aware of your environment. The more aware you are, the easier it becomes for you to pick up shifts in energies, no matter how subtle. With time, you can extrapolate beyond the present or past to the future. Being grounded is the foundation for astral projection and visits to the astral realm. Regular environmental scans will make your psychic practices more profound.

- **Cultivate Your Subconscious:** Trite, as it may sound, cultivating your subconscious is one of the best daily practices to enhance your psychic abilities. In your daily life, you are continually setting boundaries to what stimuli you ingest, whether you realize it or not. Obviously, you can't allow yourself to absorb everything you come across. This is understandable. The thing about experiences is that they are all stored within your psyche, good or bad. The quickest way to harness and hone your psychic abilities is to establish and maintain a vibrant relationship with your subconscious. This is achievable through dreams. Think of dreams as pathways into the spiritual realm. In the dream world, you are free of constraints that hold you back in the physical world. When you dream, you can explore the lands, travel anywhere, and communicate with otherworldly spirits. Through your dreams, you can become more acquainted with the subconscious realm. When this happens, you will gain access to the complete spectrum of psychic abilities. The more comfortable you become with the subconscious realm, the easier you will find it to navigate physical and spiritual realms fluidly. It may become as easy as ABC. Keep a dream journal to help you retain memories of whatever happens in dreamland.

- **Tune in with Your Chi Energy:** Energy-based activities such as Qigong and Yoga can help you stay in tune with your vital energy, which will, in turn, keep your aura bright and healthy.

- **Activating Your Pineal Gland:** By eating a clean and healthy diet every day, steering clear of fluoride, getting adequate sunlight and sleep, and meditating, you can activate your pineal gland. Keeping protective crystals with you can also help you achieve this.

Psychic abilities are some of the best gifts Mother Nature can bestow on a person. They allow you to see things beyond the plane of human existence. We all possess psychic abilities to some extent. However, most people go through life without unlocking the potentials that exist within them. If you aren't mindful, the same thing can happen to you. Psychic gifts are like any other skill that one has. If you practice consistently, you will achieve the results you seek. If everyone on earth were more in tune, we might all be able to activate our psychic powers.

Conclusion

Aura reading is not a psychic ability exclusive to a select group of people. Anybody can become an aura reader if they understand and accept what it takes. This book has taken you on an exciting journey on what aura reading entails. It covers a broad range of topics regarding aura reading. It is impossible to finish this book and put its content into practice without becoming a skilled psychic. There are different techniques to guide you through aura reading. Without a doubt, you now have everything you need to become a prolific and professional aura reader.

Let no one make you feel weird or eccentric for believing in the existence of the spiritual realm. Be confident in your belief, and always remain in tune with the cosmos. Please, do not forget that consistency and patience is the key to becoming an accomplished aura reader. As you work on your aura reading, don't forget to hone other psychic abilities! I am excited about your success!

Part 2: Telepathy

Unlocking the Secrets of Sending Telepathic Messages and Psychic Development

Introduction

As a fan of the X-Men series, my first knowledge of telepathy came from Professor X, the leader of the X-Men. If you haven't watched the movie series before or read the comics, Professor X is a character with many superhuman powers, including telepathy. He could use his mind to communicate with others. He could even go into their subconscious to discover whatever is going on there. If you haven't watched X-Men or heard of Professor X, you have likely watched Sci-Fi or occult movies where people had telepathic abilities. As a child, it all seemed so real. Then, as a teenager, I believed that telepathy was just something that TV producers made up to make their shows and movies more exciting. We all like the idea of having superhuman abilities. However, due to my inquisitiveness and knack for research, I soon learned that telepathy is real.

In basic terms, telepathy is defined as the ability to transmit information from one person to another by means beyond the known five senses. You don't use your sense of sight, touch, smell, taste, or sound when communicating with telepathy. No, the form of communication is beyond these five senses. Now, you may be wondering just how this is possible. If you are reading this right now, you probably got here because you were curious about the possibility of it all. Undoubtedly, a lot of resources claim to help people understand the concept of telepathy, especially on the internet. Unfortunately, many of these resources fall short of people's expectations. I fell victim to many unoriginal and unhelpful resources before I could finally uncover everything I know about telepathy. This prompted me to make an ultimate book guide on telepathy – a guide to help people discover their psychic powers and improve them.

Despite being around for years, the techniques of telepathy have been a well-guarded secret in spiritualism. However, following the emergence of scientific evidence showing that telepathy is indeed possible, known occultists have come forward to share their knowledge with the rest of the world. *Telepathy: Unlocking the Secrets of Sending Telepathic Messages and Psychic Development* was created to help people unravel the mystery of exchanging trans-physical messages and show them how they can unlock their inner superpower. Anyone who has little to no knowledge of the occult or psychic may find all this a little overwhelming. So, if you are a beginner, this book was written with you in mind. Using the most simplified and easily digestible language, this book tells you, in depth, everything you need to know about telepathy.

In this book, you will discover the history of telepathy and how it has evolved in mankind over the years. It explains how witches and magicians in the past honed their telepathic abilities. In short, this book will help you uncover how to communicate your thoughts, feelings, and ideas to others paranormally. Considering the amount of information available, it is safe to say that you are in for a ride of a lifetime with telepathy. Without further ado, let's get to learning all about how you can unlock your psychic powers!

Chapter One: What is Telepathy?

Psychic abilities exist in many forms. From clairvoyance to precognition to telepathy, people have manifested psychic gifts in different ways. There are various ways that you could use psychic skills in their diverse forms. Your psychic type isn't about how you sense things; instead, it is all about what you experience. Telepathy is one of such psychic types that many people possess, whether they have realized it or not.

"Tele" and "Pathe"

These are the two Greek words from which the word "telepathy" was coined. *Tele* means distant, and *pathe* means feeling. It could also mean an occurrence. From this, you can simply say that telepathy means a remote sense or occurrence. In other words, it entails "feeling" something that is quite far from you. The standard definition of telepathy is a transmission of data or information from person to person without the use of the known sensory channels. The Society of Psychical Research defined telepathy as the "paranormal passage of information from one person to another." From these definitions, you can tell that telepathy entails communicating your thoughts, feelings, ideas, and mental concepts to another person without interacting with them through your five senses or physical body. Essentially, the mind is the primary tool for communication in telepathy. Telepathy is about mind-to-mind communication.

People who are well-versed in telepathy consider it a medium for transmitting paranormal information. This means that the information cannot be scientifically proven. Yet, scientific research has shown that telepathy might just be real, even if its concept isn't embraced in the scientific community. Telepathy is of the occult. The very idea of mind-to-mind communication has been around for years, long before Hollywood started to make movies with characters that have telepathic powers. Ancient people have detailed records of telepathy both in oral and writing lore. It was then considered a natural ability possessed by all humans and a unique ability possessed by trained and gifted people. Thankfully, this is still valid today. Anybody can learn to communicate telepathically as long as they are willing. If you want to start communicating with others using your mind, you can if you will put in the effort required.

The history of telepathy is quite an interesting one. Telepathy dates back to ancient Greeks and Egyptians, even though the word wasn't coined until the late 18th century. The ancient Egyptians believed spirits could send messages from one individual to another through their dreams. The ancient Greeks also believed that dreams could be used to send messages from one person to another. The knowledge of telepathy, dreams, etc., has been preserved for years by many indigenous groups.

"Telepathy" as a word was coined in 1882 by Frederic W. H. Myers, a classical scholar and founder of the Society for Psychical Research. Initially, the phenomenon was referred to by other things such as *"thought-reading," "thought transference,"* and *"communication* des *pensées."* Myers believed that "telepathy" is a more suitable term for the phenomenon. So, it became more popular than the original expressions. Initially, the research into telepathy started in the late 18th century with Franz Anton Mesmer. Mesmer is known for popularizing the concept of mesmerism, which was also referred to as animal magnetism. Those who believed in magnetism were called magnetists. Then, magnetists found that 'magnetized' or hypnotized subjects could read magnetists' minds and even respond to m Note that I defined mind-reading as the ability to "sense" or "feel" others' thoughts and feeling mental instructions. This jumpstarted the interest in telepathy research.

Later in the 19th century, telepathy became an observed phenomenon in psychotherapy, which was still emerging. This piqued the interest of William James in the phenomenon, causing him to advocate for scientific study. Note that the Society for Psychical Research (SPR) was founded in 1884. That was when scientific study into telepathy actually started. As a matter of fact, telepathy was the first psychic ability to be observed and studied scientifically. This was done to establish a link between psychic phenomena and science. The scientific study of telepathy was the main objective in establishing the American faction of the SPR in 1885. William James was one of the American Society for Psychical Research members to conduct experiments regarding telepathy.

The early experiments were relatively simple and straightforward. They involved putting two individuals in different rooms. One person acted as the sender of numbers, words, and images. The other person served as the receiver of numbers, words, and images. Then, physiologist Charles Richet introduced chances to the tests, leading to the discovery that telepathy could occur outside of hypnotism. With the addition of mathematical chance to experiments, the tests became more advanced. Moving forward to 1930, J.B. Rhine, an American Botanist and member of Duke University, North Carolina, started the Extrasensory Perception experiments. The ESP tests involved playing cards with special symbols. The cards were initially called Zener cards and then renamed to ESP cards. Rhine found it challenging to ascertain whether the psychic communication of information happened through telepathy, precognition, or clairvoyance. He concluded that telepathy is the same psychic ability as clairvoyance, although they both manifested differently. He also discovered that distance and obstacles do not actually affect telepathic communication between the sender and receiver. Other testing methods emerged as a result of Rhine's work on telepathy. By the late 19th century, there was a minimal controversy in the scientific community surrounding the possibility of extrasensory perception.

Over the years, several theories have emerged in the bid to explain telepathy and how it works. Interestingly, none of these theories have been found adequate. This is because, just like Rhine said, psychic abilities are intermingled into one another. You simply cannot separate one from the other to quantify the elements of psychic experiences. Telepathy cannot be explained without clairvoyance, and this goes for other psychic phenomena. Despite the advancement of many theories, science is yet to gain an understanding or explanation of how telepathy works. Below is a list of characteristics that have been observed over the years. Note that these characteristics are not applicable in all cases.

- Telepathy is closely connected to the emotional states of the sender and receiver.

- Women are more inclined to be telepathic than men.

- Telepathic abilities may become enhanced with age, possibly because the five physical senses weaken with age. This sharpens the telepathic faculty of a person.

- Telepathy is more easily induced in the dream state.

- Specific biological changes occur during telepathy. For instance, the receiver's brain waves match those of the sender when sharing a telepathic message.

- Telepathy is heightened during the full moon. This suggests that the cosmic energy field plays a part in the telepathic sending and receiving of messages.

As Rhine said, psychic skills known to humans are all blended into one another. Personally, I consider telepathy as someone "hearing" another person's thoughts. In the psychic world, this is referred to as *clairaudience*, which basically means clear hearing. Clairvoyance is the psychic ability that involves sensing or seeing another person's thoughts, feelings, etc., *Clairsentience* is the ability to "feel" a person's thoughts, feelings, etc., Note that one similarity with these psychic abilities is that they all have to do with gaining access to information about another person paranormally. This shows that these skills do indeed blend into one another.

Being a paranormal ability that usually isn't associated with humans, one might expect that people wouldn't believe in the existence of telepathy or any other psychic ability. Over the years, there have been proven cases of psychic fraud. Many people who claimed to possess psychic powers have been proven to be liars and fraudsters who deceived people for selfish reasons. Despite these cases, many people still believe that psychic abilities, such as telepathy and clairvoyance exist. There are reasons for this. Recently, a report found that psychic believers tend to think less objectively or analytically. This means that they tend to view things from a personal perspective, which I wouldn't call a bad thing. Another reason people believe in psychic abilities is due to the existence of positive scientific research findings. Due to mixed evidence from the scientific community, believers in psychic abilities have reasons to accept that the claims are genuine and real. As long as there continue to be cases that suggest that these abilities are real or possible, believers will continue to believe. This doesn't necessarily portray something wrong.

Telepathy isn't just considered as the ability to communicate thoughts and ideas. It is also believed that telepathy can be used to influence the thoughts and ideas of others. When this happens, telepathy becomes mind control. Having given insight into telepathy's history and the scientific concerns surrounding the phenomena, the subsequent chapters focus on unraveling telepathy's secrets and how it works according to the occult.

Chapter Two: Types of Telepathy

Telepathy is a combination of different psychic activities, all of which center on the mind. Usually, when you think of communication, you think about oral and nonverbal communication through writing or speaking. But as I have established, telepathy is communication through the mind. If you think of superheroes and aliens when you hear about telepathy, that is quite okay. The reality is, however, different. You don't necessarily need a cape to have that ability to communicate with others using your mind. Telepathy is a skill that you already possess, even if you don't know it yet. That is why the purpose of this book is to help you "unlock" your gifts. Telepathy is more natural than you probably think. Everyone has the innate ability to tune into the consciousness of others to share messages with them.

Telepathic activities vary from person to person. Four widely acknowledged telepathic activities manifest in humans. These are:

- Mind-reading – being able to sense or hear what is happening in the mind of others.

- Mental communication – directly communicating with others without words or gestures.

- Telepathic impression – planting words or thoughts into the mind of another person. One could also plant an image.

- Mind control- being able to influence and control another person's actions by controlling their thoughts.

For you to fully understand telepathy, you must understand human consciousness beyond the surface level. You must understand on a much deeper level. Humans generally have a consciousness, which is essentially the awareness of feelings. Consciousness is the basis of every human experience. When you understand human consciousness deeply, you will also understand that it is possible to connect with others' consciousness. You do this by aligning your consciousness grid with that of a person you choose. Another way to understand this is to look at it from an energy perspective. Humans vibrate energy. Every human has an energy field, also referred to as the aura, surrounding them. Through the aura, you can transmit frequencies from your energy field to another person. When your vibrational frequency aligns with that of another person, it becomes possible to communicate telepathically with that person. This way, you don't need your senses to communicate since you have established an auric connection.

As a matter of fact, psychic skills, such as clairvoyance, clairsentience, and clairaudience are activated through a comprehension of the auric field. And since I have already established that these abilities are all connected to telepathy one way or another, it makes sense that the vibrating energy field also plays a role in telepathic communication. Many people believe that psychics are the only ones with these abilities, but that isn't true. Psychics are not very different from you. They don't necessarily possess special skills beyond what is present in everyone. However, the difference is that psychics have put in the required effort to hone and enhance their skills. Thus, it has become more natural for them.

Let's take a more in-depth look at the four most common telepathic activities listed earlier.

Mind Reading

The simplest way to define or think of mind-reading is as an intuitive ability to know the unspoken thoughts. Mind-reading is one of the most common telepathic activities that many people engage in, knowingly or unknowingly. Without a doubt, you have had at least one instance where you knew what was on someone's mind without them telling you. Or it could be that another person told you something you were thinking about without you telling them what it was. This experience isn't limited to just you or a handful of people. The experience is quite common. Reading people's thoughts starts with reading people themselves. The better you are at reading people, the better you become at mind-reading. By learning to pay attention to the little, seemingly trivial things people express with their physical bodies and words, you can learn to discover what isn't being said with the mouth or body. To an extent, you have probably read what is on a person's mind without meaning to. Subconsciously, humans observe and pick up certain things about other people. But since the effort is subconscious and sometimes unconscious, we don't pay mind to this ability; many people even cast the possibility aside.

Mind-reading is an innate ability – it is inbuilt in everyone. However, suppose you do not train yourself and focus on using this skill consciously. In that case, the ability cannot be fully developed to the point where you can pull it off confidently. Individuals who have mastered the art of mind-reading can mirror the thoughts and feelings of people they meet and interact with. Note that I defined mind-reading as the ability to "sense" or "feel" others' thoughts and feelings. This means that you don't have to hear the thoughts in your own head, but you can tell what they are. Sensing another person's thoughts and feelings is possible in a couple of ways. But the easiest way is to focus on the person whose thoughts you want to read and attempt to empathize with them. Simply put, you put yourself in that person's shoes. By doing this, you can tell the state of mind of a person.

To read another's mind is easy if you understand certain things. The first thing to understand is that you cannot read another person's mind unless you open your spirit up. Mind-reading requires opening up your aura to the people around you. Certain things, stress, frustration, anxiety, etc., often obstruct one from opening up to others. To overcome the obstruction, you must be grounded in the moment. This means that you have to let go of all thoughts and feelings, leaving your mind empty to accommodate another mind's information. Be keen to soak up the surrounding energy while keeping your own thoughts at bay. Then, you also need to "see" the other person. In this sense, seeing them means being conscious of their energy and frequency. This will give you much-needed insight into their situation. Finally, you have to focus on them. Focusing allows you to connect with their energies and subtle bodies, revealing a lot about that person.

Mental Communication

This is direct communication with another person without the use of words or bodily gestures. Mental communication is what most people consider telepathy; they neglect other aspects, including mind-reading, impression, and control. Mind-to-mind communication occurs in ordinary ways in our everyday life. You might have mentally communicated with another person without paying attention to it. It is common sense that humans are always in touch with each other through mental communication in our everyday interactions. Every day, we send and receive thoughts, feelings, messages, and information beyond the five physical senses, which are supposed to be the mediums of communication. Surely, you have heard someone say they are "in touch" with their loved ones. When people say this, it may seem as though they are merely saying it for no reason, but that isn't the case.

One can pick up on the thoughts, feelings, moods, and desires of a loved one regardless of distance and other factors. For instance, a mother can tell when her child hundreds of miles away is in some sort of danger. How is this possible? Undoubtedly, it is possible to pick up on another's internal state by reading their facial expressions, body language, tone of voice, etc., But the fact is that you also frequently communicate with others on extra- physical levels, i.e., beyond what is observable on the physical level. You are not yet attuned to the activity consciously. Have you ever had someone in mind and then received a call from them shortly thereafter? How often do you enter a room and can immediately tell that someone in that room doesn't like you?

Mental communication manifests in different ways. Contrary to what you may think, your thoughts are tangible. They do have form, but not in a rigid way like things in the physical world. Thoughts can be perceived and transmitted beyond the physical senses. Depending on your perception, thoughts can even assume shapes and colors. They are always moving, shifting, and changing in ways beyond ordinary understanding. However, the present state of the world has made it even harder to mentally communicate with others. In the modern world, we are disconnected from nature, addicted to technology, and our psyches are continually being bombarded with all sorts of marketing and information. All of this makes it incredibly difficult to tune in with our extra physical senses to communicate with one another. It hinders our ability to connect and remain in touch with one another, intuitively and empathically. For indigenous people who have managed to preserve the structural integrity of their culture, mental communication and telepathy as a whole are a normal part of their daily experiences. As a result, those who choose to be shamans or psychics can develop these abilities to levels that may seem extraordinary. The ability is enhanced and developed through one's immersion in complementary spiritual practices. Like any other skill, it can be improved with practice and focus.

Telepathic impression actually falls under mental communication. It involves planting words, thoughts, and even ideas into another's mind. Psychologically, this may be referred to as a manipulation technique. Still, it really depends on the kind of information you plant. Also, this is done telepathically. Manipulation in psychology often involves suggesting thoughts and ideas into another's mind through oral communication. Telepathic impression, on the other hand, is done without the use of words or anything related. One simply projects an image, a word, or an idea in the mind of another individual so that they see it exactly as it is in the sender's mind.

Telepathic Mind Control

Telepathy can also be used to influence or control the thoughts and feelings of another person. When you control or influence another with your mind, it is called mind control. In itself, mind control is a loose term. It can be used in different contexts. When you think of mind control, the first thing that probably comes to mind is other people's enslavement. Even in movies and TV shows, mind control is used to make puppets and robots out of people. However, this only happens in fictional settings. In reality, what comes close to mind control, as portrayed in the movies, is found in certain religious practices, specifically the high-demand ones such as cults and ideological organizations. In these practices, they use extreme sleep deprivation, hypnosis, mind-altering drugs, gaslighting, subliminal influencing, etc., to control and influence members' thoughts and feelings. In most cases, these methods actually do work, but only if they are applied collectively. Individually, they cannot actually control the thoughts and feelings of another.

Telepathically, though, it is quite possible to influence people's thoughts by planting other things in their minds. When you telepathically control someone else's thoughts, you are inadvertently controlling their actions. This is because thoughts predict actions. Unfortunately, malevolent people attempt to try telepathic mind control on others at night when they are sleeping. They do this because during a person's sleep it is much easier to exert control over their mind. Telepathic mind control is all about influence. It can be achieved with or without the use of external strategies or props. It can be beneficial or destructive, depending on the person involved. When used positively, telepathic mind control can help facilitate beneficial life changes.

On the other hand, it can also destroy a person when used negatively. As I said, this all depends on the person asserting influence over someone else's mind. This is why indigenous people have tried to limit telepathy's knowledge to people who are thought to be pure of heart.

Many people believe that these four telepathic activities are the types of telepathy, but this is not so, which is why I explained these four first. Contrary to this common misconception, there are three types of telepathy: *instinctual telepathy, mental telepathy,* and *spiritual telepathy.* Some people also consider animal telepathy a type of telepathy. Instinctual and mental telepathy have both been supported by scientific studies dating back to the 19th century. Spiritual telepathy is best explained from a spiritual perspective.

One by one, let's delve into the four types of telepathy.

Instinctual Telepathy

Have your "guts" ever told you something that turned out to be true? If you have ever had a feeling or thought about someone that ended up being correct, that is referred to as a "gut" feeling because it comes from somewhere inside you. A "gut" feeling is a perfect example or manifestation of instinctual telepathy. Instinctual telepathy is the most common type of telepathy. This is the kind of telepathy that humans share with animals. Instinctual telepathy is still commonly used as a form of communication among indigenous people. It is a form of communication through the solar-plexus chakra, which is the chakra of emotion and instinct. Hawaiian native priests, popularly referred to as the Kahunas, believe that the solar plexus is the origin of instinctual telepathy. They believe that telepathic messages are sent and received by people through the solar plexus. For you to achieve instinctual telepathy with another person, your solar plexus has to send out the message, which is then detected by the recipient's solar plexus. The Kahunas also believe that one person's etheric body sends out a silver, sticky thread to the solar plexus of another person, establishing a connection between them. Telepathic messages are then sent through the connecting thread. According to the Kahunas, the telepathic message is first received by the low self, which is also the instinctual self. The "low" self is called the Unhipili. From the low self, the message is relayed to the Uhane, the middle or rational self. Finally, the message rises to the mind and becomes somewhat of a memory. When repeated telepathic communication happens between two people like this, the silver thread eventually becomes a cord, and the etheric cord results in strong telepathic communication between two or more persons. You can send the cords from your etheric body to strangers with a simple handshake or a glance.

Interestingly, indigenous people of other cultures hold similar beliefs to the Kahunas of Hawaii. The Kalahari bushmen of Africa believe that a belly button wire connects humans and other living creatures. They believe that this wire is a silver-like stream of energy that is present in all creatures. Through the wire, the Kalahari bushmen were able to send and receive messages telepathically. The Australian Aboriginals believe their *miwi* makes it possible for them to communicate from a distance. The miwi is said to be located in the pit of the stomach. Roughly, it translates to "instinct" or "soul." It is also believed that the miwi makes it possible to predict the future. Like the Hawaiian Kahunas, the Japanese also believe that the solar plexus makes instinctive, nonverbal communication possible. They believe that their *haragei* makes it possible to know the intentions of others. Haragei translates to "guts" in English. Japanese businessmen trust in their haragei when making business decisions. If their haragei doesn't connect with the other person's, they will likely call off a business deal. The western culture uses gut feeling to describe this phenomenon as experienced by the Kahunas, Kalahari bushmen, Australian Aboriginals, and Japanese.

You have likely had at least one situation where you have trusted your gut when trying to make a decision. There must also have been instances where your guts simply don't want you to trust another person. These gut feelings are all instances of instinctual telepathy. As I said, instinctual telepathy uses the solar plexus chakra, which is the third energy center in the energy system. Instinctual telepathy allows you to sense the feelings and needs of another person from a distance. Typical instances of instinctual telepathy often occur between people who share strong emotional bonds, such as lovers, married couples, best friends, twins, parents, and children.

Example: You want something for your birthday, something specific, such as a chain with your name engraved on it. You don't tell anybody because you want them to get you whatever they can afford. To your surprise, your best friend gets you the exact thing you thought about as your birthday gift. When you ask them, they tell you, "I just felt like this is what you would want." This is instinctual telepathy at its finest. Your best friend was able to sense your desire and need. You communicated it to them telepathically.

Mental Telepathy

Mental telepathy is what we all commonly think of as telepathy. Most people don't know of any other type of telepathy. Mental telepathy is mind-to-mind telepathy. This kind of telepathy uses the throat chakra for communication. It takes place in the lower levels of the mental plane, located in the auric field. To practice true mental telepathy, you need a focused, one-way center of attention. Mental telepathy is often mistaken for trance channeling. Trance channeling is a form of mediumship in which an entity takes charge of a channel's body to pass across a message. Mental telepathy, on the other hand, happens between two conscious and focused minds. Mind-reading, mental communication, telepathic impressing, and telepathic mind control are mental telepathy forms.

There are two widely-known examples of mental telepathy that are popularly discussed in esoteric and scientific settings. These examples are from the works of Alice Bailey, Helena Roerich, and Helena Blavatsky. Each of these women was believed to have worked with a group of Tibetan monks from the Himalayas. These women functioned as amanuensis for the Tibetan masters. Their books, particularly those of Helena Blavatsky, were very influential in esoterism and science. In fact, Albert Einstein was said to be an admirer of the works of Blavatsky. Helena Roerich was said to have communicated with Tibetan master Morya to create spiritual philosophy books through mental telepathy. Alice Bailey worked with Tibetan Master Djwal Khul to create nineteen books discussing consciousness and human evolution.

When she was 15, Bailey received a visit from the master who said he would have work for her in the future. Twenty-four years later, Bailey heard a "voice" inside her head, asking her to help write and produce a series of books. Reluctantly, she agreed. Initially, Bailey could only listen and write the words as they appeared in her brain individually. Over time, as their souls became attuned, she gained direct access to the master's thoughts and ideas. Over thirty years, she worked with Morya to create a series of nineteen books. Bailey is responsible for introducing New Age concepts into pop culture.

Real mental telepathy, unfortunately, is rare in the modern day. For one to achieve real mental telepathy, they must become attuned with their subconscious. Note that mental telepathy can be spontaneous or deliberate. We see instances of spontaneous mental telepathy every day. If you and another person have ever said the same thing simultaneously, that is spontaneous mental telepathy. However, deliberate mental telepathy is achievable by people who choose to focus on practicing telepathy with intent.

Spiritual Telepathy

Spiritual telepathy is also known as soul-to-soul telepathy. This is the highest and most advanced form of telepathy. It is also the most difficult to achieve. Soul-to-soul telepathy happens from the crown chakra and from the highest levels of the mental plane. It becomes possible only when you have successfully established a connection between your brain, mind, and soul. When you align your brain, mind, and soul, you become an intermediary between the physical and spiritual realms. Spiritual beings, such as angels, spirit guides, and the Divine cannot directly affect anything in the material world. Instead, they require people with a direct communication link between their brain and soul. They can then impress information, thoughts, and ideas via the soul, which is then relayed and impressed on the brain.

Without a soul connection, spiritual telepathy is impossible. A soul connection can be described as a cord through which spiritual energy flows from two souls' energy centers on the spiritual plane. You can think of soul connection as a wire that allows energy to flow from one soul to another. An example of the soul connection is the twin flame cord, which makes telepathy possible between twins. But this isn't the only recognized type of soul connection that exists among humans. Everyone has pre-existing soul connections with people with whom they share a soul group. The soul connections remain dormant until you meet people in your soul group. When you meet them, the soul connection activates, making telepathic communication possible and easy. Through your soul connection, you can send and receive energy with one another. This significantly increases your ability to put yourselves in one another's shoes, which is part of what telepathy encompasses. The potential for spiritual telepathy is one of the benefits of sharing spiritual energy through soul connection.

Animal Telepathy

Some people can communicate telepathically with animals. Animals also communicate with one another telepathically. Telepathic communication between two humans isn't so different from telepathic communication between humans and animals. They both happen through the mind. Since animals cannot communicate verbally but still find a way to send and receive messages among one another, it is believed that telepathy is the language of the animal kingdom. Although many people don't realize it, animals are sentient beings. They have their own desires, purposes, and choices to communicate with people who are willing to listen or pay attention. Animal communicators can telepathically communicate with animals to determine their thoughts, feelings, needs, and desires. A lot of people go to animal communicators to help them interact with their pets. If you master the telepathy techniques in this book, you can also start communicating with your pet telepathically.

Don't forget that mental telepathy is the focus of this book. It entails four activities: reading, communicating, impressing, and control. Throughout this book, you will discover how to practice each of these telepathic activities.

Chapter Three: The Benefits of Using Telepathy

Psychic abilities have many benefits; that is why some people choose to call them gifts. Naturally, the more receptive you become to psychic communication, the more advanced you become emotionally, mentally, and spiritually. Limiting your ability to send and receive information to your five senses is akin to limiting yourself as an individual. Advancing your communication beyond your five senses can improve all aspects of your life, from your relationships to finances and awareness. As strange as this may seem to you, your relationships' problems can be fixed from enhanced psychic awareness. Telepathy makes communication more effective, lessening the possibility of misinterpretation or misunderstanding. Words can be misinterpreted, but if you plant a piece of information from your own head inside another person's mind, regardless of who that person is, you are more likely to be understood as you want.

Every human being has a bank of higher intelligence accessible to them when they become more psychically aware. This higher intelligence exceeds the scope of our personal reasoning. As a matter of fact, personal reasoning is one of the limitations you suffer from as a human being. When you unlock the higher intelligence that comes with being psychically aware, you can apply it to different aspects of your life. For example, let's say that you notice your partner is uncomfortable. You try to figure out the cause, but you can't find out what it is. Suppose you are telepathically able and receptive to your psychic senses. In that case, you have a greater chance of seeing the cause of their discomfort. You can easily read their mind to find out precisely what is wrong, but that is not all. You also have the opportunity to find out the perfect solution to the problem. There are more ways telepathy (or any other psychic ability) can help you improve your personal, social, professional, and spiritual life. Let's find out what they are.

1. Improved Communication

As you develop your telepathic ability, your communication skills improve. Not just with yourself, but also with the people around you. Greater and improved communication is one of the foremost benefits of telepathy. There are potentials in developing your telepathy skills. Think of how incredible it would be if you could just look at a person and find out certain things about them. How incredible would it be if you could read someone's mind and find out things about them that could improve your relationship with them? With telepathy, you can determine precisely how a person feels rather than how they tell you they feel. You can also find out the cause(s) of their emotions, whether positive or negative. When you meet someone new, you can use your telepathic skills to find out everything they have been through in life. This will help you ascertain the best approach to take in interacting with them.

Imagine being able to know precisely when your loved one needs support or anything else from you. Think about how it will make the people around you feel if you know just the right thing to say to them at any time, even if you are only meeting them for the first time. There is a level of intimacy that is only achievable with other people when effective communication is in place. Telepathy makes you emotionally intelligent. When you can tell the exact emotion a person is feeling, you also know how best to respond to them. This, precisely, is what emotional intelligence entails.

2. Telepathy Improves your Accuracy

This goes back to the first benefit of telepathy, which is improved communication. Telepathy is unquestionably more accurate than any other form of communication. It is also more accurate than language. This is because telepathy can convey even the abstracts and synthesis - which are usually pretty tricky with language. Language, whether written or spoken, is suitable for sharing lower frequency messages with a linear structure. The more detailed information is, the harder it is to communicate it effectively to the average human being. Oral or written communication can become subjective no matter how objective you try to be with your choice of words and grammar. For instance, you might say something to someone, and they would see it differently from how you had it in your mind. This is one reason why communication through language tends to cause conflict regardless of the communicators' intentions.

Telepathy, on the other hand, improves the accuracy of information. It can convey reality precisely as it is in the mind of a communicator. If you want to tell someone something and you don't want them to misunderstand you, all you need to do is plant the image of what you mean exactly as it is in your mind. Doing this leaves no room for misinterpretation. Or you can simply send a direct mind-to-mind message which would be impossible to dispute. Either way, you are bound to be more accurate in how you convey and relay information to the people around you. This goes the other way for people communicating with you as well. A world where everyone can send and receive information directly through their mind is an enviable one.

3. Send and Receive Large Amounts of Data

This is another benefit of telepathy that is particularly fascinating when you think about it. Telepathy provides humans an opportunity to exchange extensive data easily, regardless of the size. And the most exciting thing is that exchanging multidimensional data also becomes easy. As the famous saying goes, "A picture is worth a thousand words." In which case, impressing information on the mind is undoubtedly a thousand pictures! Through a mental impression, you can easily exchange multidimensional data layers that can include anything from language to sound and image. One may also exchange other forms of information that humans have not yet known or identified. The current form of communication through language has been limiting us from experiencing the vast amount of data beyond the reach of language descriptions. Telepathy presents an opportunity to improve the capacity and quality of communication globally. This is one reason to be thankful that telepathy is a skill that can be learned by anyone.

4. Increased Vibrations

To unlock your telepathy skills, meditation is one thing you must include in your daily routine. Meditation has been proven to raise vibrations. You already know that everything in existence is made up of energy. There is one significant source of energy that connects everyone in the cosmos. This energy also flows through everything. Now, energy exists on a spectrum. This spectrum is made up of frequencies which we call vibrations. On one side of the spectrum, you have the low vibrations. These are dense frequencies that are associated with negative feelings and emotions, such as anger and envy. At the other end of the spectrum, you have the high vibrations, frequencies associated with positive feelings and emotions such as love and happiness. When you are on the spectrum's high vibration side, it means that the energy flowing through you is that of love and joy. This is the same energy in which Higher Beings exist. This is also the frequency on which you can find your higher self; it is where your soul lives. Actually, everyone has their higher selves in the high vibrational state. This means that being in a high vibrational state allows you to connect with your higher self and the universe's collective consciousness. This gives you access to information from the angels, spirit guides, ascended masters, and even the Divine.

Telepathy requires daily meditation to keep you in the right mindset for the use of your psychic skills. Meditation helps you reach the high vibrational state that you need to access your psychic abilities. When you are in that high vibrational state, your psychic portals become open, and your vibrations are at the maximum level. In a way, this becomes a cycle. The more you practice telepathy, the closer you reach the highest end of the energy spectrum. And the closer you are to the high vibrational state, the better you become at using your telepathy skills, as well as other psychic skills. It is a win-win situation for you since you need to reach a high vibrational state to develop your skills more.

5. Opens your Energy Centers

Your seven chakras make up your energy centers. They are the portals through which energy flows from the energy field to your physical body. Healthy and balanced chakras are vital for your physical, mental, emotional, and spiritual wellbeing. Chakras are essential. Without them, you cannot use any psychic ability you have. In fact, you need to keep your chakras open and balanced at all times if you want to be able to communicate psychically. Your chakras are directly linked to your psychic portals. Remember what I said about the Kahunas' and Japanese belief in the solar plexus being responsible for distant communication? Well, there is a solar plexus chakra linked to the solar plexus, and when this chakra is open, it makes you clairsentient. This means that you will be able to sense the thoughts, feelings, and needs of another person psychically. As I already established, telepathy is linked with other psychic skills, such as clairvoyance, clairsentience, and clairaudience. Without these other four skills, it is safe to say that you might find telepathy difficult or impossible. The good thing is that you are unlikely to have one of these skills without possessing the others.

To open up your psychic portals, you have to work on clearing your chakras and ensuring they remain opened and balanced at all times. This is achievable through meditation. Chakra meditations are essential for keeping your chakras balanced and healthy. Telepathy practice requires you to do chakra meditation to keep your chakras, especially your third-eye chakra, open. In this way, telepathy helps you keep your energy centers open. This means that energy will continue to flow to your physical body through the energy centers, keeping you in a healthy and vibrant state. The more you practice your telepathy skills, the more your physical, mental, emotional, and spiritual wellbeing improves. If there is one way to ensure your psychic portals stay open, it is the regular use your psychic gifts.

6. Awareness and Discovery

Like all psychic abilities, telepathy improves your awareness of yourself. But not only does it lead to self-discovery, but it also makes you more aware of other people. When you are telepathic, you have an opportunity to connect the patterns of your actions to the emotions you feel deep inside you. This applies to the people you interact with, too. Self-discovery is something everyone must go through in their journey on earth. Being telepathic makes self-discovery easier. Telepathy requires you to be more in tune with your consciousness. That is precisely what you need to discover yourself and become more aware of yourself. When self-discovery and self-awareness happen, it results in self-confidence. Developing the psychic part of yourself is all you need to become more confident in yourself and your purpose on earth. It makes it easier for you to face and overcome any challenges.

Let's say that you have sharpened your telepathic skills from mind-reading to mental communication, impressing, and control. So, you meet someone you are trying to do a deal with. Unknown to you, this person has something else – something negative – planned for you. Unknown to them, you can read their mind. So, you read their mind and find out their thoughts and feelings about you. With this knowledge, you can quickly call off the deal. By doing this, you have used your ability to overcome a challenge that could have prevented you from fulfilling a purpose. Telepathy gives you validation for your feelings and thoughts. If you feel negatively about someone that appears to be nice and friendly, you might blame yourself for feeling that way about them. However, if you use your telepathic gift to scan their mind, you will be able to find out why you feel that way about them. This gives you validation for your feelings. No matter how kind a person may seem, if your guts don't accept them, chances are you should be wary.

7. Prepares you to Receive Spirit Messages

Telepathy requires you to be present in the moment. This is achieved through meditation sessions. When you meditate, you are putting your mind in a state of calm and peace. The whole point of meditating to awaken and enhance your telepathic skills is to calm your mind for what it is about to send or receive. This is highly vital for connecting with your higher consciousness or Spirit. You have to enter this state if you want to use spiritual telepathy to receive messages from the spiritual plane. These messages can be anything from guidance to a warning. Why do you need to achieve a calm state of mind before you receive spirit messages? It is straightforward.

Imagine that you are in a crowded room and you see a person you know across the room. You wave and try to say hello to them, but this person doesn't wave or say anything back. Obviously, they cannot see or hear you because the room is crowded. Now, imagine you are in the same room without anybody except you and that person. They will be able to see and hear you immediately when you enter the room. This is how telepathy and meditation work. Without regular meditation, it would be impossible to send and receive telepathic messages. You cannot exchange information if your mind is chaotic; the message would be disrupted, and you wouldn't be able to make any sense of it. However, when the mind is quiet, it means your mind is in the necessary space for the Spirit to send you messages. Mental chatter makes it impossible to receive guidance from the Higher plane. By regularly practicing mental telepathy with people around you, you open yourself to the possibility of spiritual telepathy. Regular use of your telepathic ability means that your mind will remain in a constant state of calm and peace. This is precisely what you need to connect with the collective consciousness. Telepathy is an effective way of connecting with the Spirit and receiving guidance and other helpful information.

8. Opportunity to Explore the Higher Planes

When you are finally able to strike a connection with the Spirit by regularly practicing your psychic skill, you become open to the possibility of visiting and exploring the spiritual realms. As I have made clear, telepathy requires you to be attuned with your consciousness and the collective consciousness of the universe. Reaching this state opens you up to several opportunities that other people are not privileged to. There are certain places that your physical body cannot visit, no matter what. However, your soul or spirit can visit the places. Before your spirit can gain access to these places, though, you need to be in a high vibrational state. As established, telepathy practice is useful in increasing your vibrations, which means you have a higher chance of connecting with your soul. With your soul, you can then explore the spiritual realms and gain access to critical information. You can meet with angels, masters, spirit guides, etc., There is much to learn about yourself and the cosmos as a whole when you visit the spiritual realms. If you don't do certain things that telepathy practice requires you to do, you may not achieve any of them.

---

9. Improved Relationships

What would your relationships be like if you could communicate effectively and accurately with literally no hitch? What would they be like if you were in tune with yourself and always present in the moment? How would you like your relationships if you could solve any problem by directly finding out what is on the other person's mind? When all this is possible, the end result is improved relationships. One of the best ways to improve your relationships with people is to work on your emotional intelligence skills. There are tons of books on emotional intelligence, but you don't really need these books. Emotional intelligence is one of the things that come with being telepathic. Your relationship with people, plants, animals, and other creatures in existence will significantly improve when you can telepathically create a connection with them.

10. Transparency

Total transparency becomes achievable when everyone can use telepathy. As established, telepathy makes it possible for us to understand one another in the most extraordinary capacity possible. There will be no limitations or obstructions to communication when everyone is in tune with their telepathic self. When this happens, it means that there will be complete transparency of everyone's thoughts, feelings, and actions. This might seem terrifying when you think of it at first. After all, what could be more terrifying than everyone having access to everyone else's minds at will? The thought of the person beside you being able to see your every thought is indeed scary. However, this fear will quickly fade away when you realize that life will get better if everyone isn't always trying to make sense of the world around them and the people in it. Once you understand the real reasons why people want certain things, such as money, power, or status, you may even be able to help them heal from their obsession with worldly things.

Telepathy has plenty of other benefits that will become apparent to you once you start honing your skill and using the gift.

How would you know if you have the gift of telepathy? Everyone has this gift latently or otherwise; but not everyone knows what to look out for. The next chapter gives you ten signs to look out for if you want to know whether you are a gifted telepath.

Chapter Four: Ten Signs You Have the Gift

People like to think of telepathy as an isolated psychic gift, separate from clairvoyance and other abilities. This isn't the right way to think of telepathy. To be a true telepath, you have to be clairvoyant, clairsentient, claircognizant, etc., Also, most people think that telepathy is a difficult ability that isn't learnable by the average person. Again, this is wrong. To an extent, everyone has some level of psychic skills, including telepathy, present in them. For instance, when you meet strangers, you automatically connect with their energy first. Even when you haven't met someone, your auras can still connect. This is why you can connect with someone you have only talked to through the phone. We enter each other's aura even before we physically meet. You don't know it yet, but telepathy has a role to play in the way you connect with people.

People you meet in your future are people that your inner self has already established a telepathic connection with, probably because you share the same soul group. Before you meet someone new, your inner self has already contacted them telepathically. This happens subconsciously, so, of course, you are unaware when it happens. To some extent, you only become friends with those individuals that share certain similarities with you. The similarities between you and your friends are transmitted and made possible firstly through your energetic connection; then, this connection establishes a telepathic link through which similarities are exchanged.

Most people develop their psychic abilities in childhood. In fact, psychic abilities are more prominent in children most times. In childhood, one is in an age of innocence that makes it easier to perceive psychic sensations. The older you get, the more difficult it becomes unless you practice consistently and remain in tune with your inner self. Psychic gifts may be passed down through intimate friends or relatives. Directly or indirectly, a close loved one can teach you psychic skills. Sometimes, though, one cultivates psychic skills in response to stimuli in the environment. As a child, you see more, feel more, and hear more. Keep in mind there are basic instincts that exist to help you survive your environment. But as you grow up, you become less sensitive to your environment. Certain beliefs you cultivate during the period of growth from child to adult also help reduce your connection with the world around you. Through conditioning, you subconsciously repress your psychic gifts and become fully immersed in the physical realm. You may come to accept the physical world as the only realm of reality. The good thing is that your psychic gifts only become repressed; they don't become completely lost. Occasionally, the gifts might present a glimpse before your eyes. For instance, you might sense another person's needs before they even say them out loud and then wonder how you were able to know.

There is no definitive way with which telepathic abilities manifest in people. But there are some common ways. For one, some people are simply born as clairsentients. People like this just have a clear sense of knowing all things. They just know things even when they don't mean to. Some are born with a clear sense of seeing; these people are referred to as clairvoyants. They may be able to see spirits and otherworldly beings because of their ability. When you are born as a clairvoyant or clairsentient, you are more inclined to have the gift of telepathy. Some also have the clairaudience gift – the ability to perceive stimuli beyond the sense of hearing. A clairaudient can "hear" things without necessarily using their ears. One thing that is common with these psychic skills is the use of senses beyond the physical ones we all know. Essentially, this is the basis of telepathy – communicating without the use of the five senses. The point is that having any of these gifts makes you inclined to the gift of telepathy. In some cases, when the gift has been repressed, a life-changing event may awaken that part of you. Once this happens, you become open to exploring your gift.

There are several ways that your psychic gift can become apparent to you. You might have even used mental telepathy before and become confused as to how that was possible. Well, thankfully, there are ways you can tell if you have telepathic or psychic gifts. Below are ten of the most common ways to tell if you have the telepathy gift. Some of them have examples to help you better understand and see if you have been in a similar situation before.

1. Your Gut Feelings are Super Strong

Everyone experiences gut feelings, which is the ability to sense or feel something about a person or a situation. What you sense may be good or bad, depending on the person or the situation. Suppose your instinct is often accurate about a person, event, or anything. In that case, it means that you have powerful gut feelings. It also means that you may have telepathy and/or other psychic abilities. Your gut feelings as a telepath are quite different from that of an ordinary person. The pull is usually more substantial. As a telepath, you are more sensitive to perceptions and sensations around you. This explains how a telepath can tell when a loved one in another location is in danger or something similar. Your psychic pull is more vigorous and clearer than most people's. If you have ever felt like you were being pulled towards a specific direction, together with a clear sense of knowing it was happening, then you may be telepathic. Plus, ordinary people only have gut feelings randomly and occasionally. Being a telepath means that your instinctive self is ever at alert. Instinctual telepathy is like a regular thing for you when you have the gift. Now, when you start exploring your psychic gift, you become open to other types of telepathy, such as spiritual telepathy or animal telepathy. See an example of how this sign of telepathy may manifest.

Example: Your best friend has just met a new person they seem interested in dating. Of course, you have to meet this person; so, your best friend chooses a date when you can get to know them. On the D-day, you are at the meeting venue, and your friend arrives with their new partner. You immediately get a strange feeling about

---

this new person. You don't know what it is, but you feel like you can't just trust them. You don't want to upset your friend, so you decide to keep your feeling to yourself. Eventually, your friend finds out that their new partner isn't who they claimed to be. Your gut feeling about them was proven right.

2. You Accurately Predict Things That Haven't Happened

It is one thing to have a strong gut feeling about a person or a situation, but predicting the future is entirely different. If you can predict things before they happen, you have powerful psychic gifts, and you just might be a telepath. Predicting the future is one of the most prominent signs in people with a psychic gift. Additionally, if the things you predict turn out to be right most times, it becomes even more apparent that you have the gift. In this context, predicting the future doesn't necessarily mean that you have to give a detailed, scene-by-scene narration of something yet to happen. You don't have to; the small occurrences and predictions count as well.

Example: The day is bright and clear. The sun is shining radiantly, and there are no clouds. Yet, you have a strong feeling it will be raining soon. Your mother is just preparing to leave the house. You turn to her and tell her to take an umbrella with her; she laughs at you and says the sky is too clear for it to rain. You smile back and think, "She's probably right." Your mother leaves the house, and you retire to your room to get some homework done. No more than thirty minutes later, the clouds grow dark and the sun vanishes from sight. The clouds gather; it starts drizzling, and before you know it, the rain starts beating down hard.

This may seem like something out of a supernatural movie. Still, if something like that happens to you, you may have some psychic abilities that you need to pay more attention to.

3. Your Dreams are Vivid

Have you ever had a dream where everything felt so real that the dream didn't go away for days? This kind of dream is referred to as a lucid dream. If you know anything about lucid dreams, then you probably know that they have always been tied to psychic gifts. It is easier to visit the spiritual plane when you have a lucid dream. When one is in the sleep state, there is little or no resistance. This means that your mind cannot interfere with what comes to you in your dream. Dreamland is the best place to receive intuitive hits. The more you open up, the easier it becomes for you to attain higher consciousness places, such as a lucid dream state. Dream in this context does not only refer to when you sleep at night. You may also have vivid daydreams. If you regularly have lucid dreams, you may have strong psychic powers that are begging to be unlocked. Pay attention to your dreams.

Example: You are watching the TV in your living room. There is a movie playing, but you feel yourself start to drift to sleep. You struggle to keep your eyes open, but before you know it, you are far off in dreamland. While in dreamland, you dream of a friend from high school. You haven't seen this friend in a while. Soon, you wake up from sleep and remember your dream. You find it amusing that you would dream of this person even though you haven't seen them in a while. Throughout the rest of the day, you weren't able to shake them off your mind. You wonder why, but you pay no attention to it. The next day, you come across this person on your way to work!

4. You are Extra Receptive to Sensory Input

This is a common thing with people who have one psychic gift or the other. So, if you are a telepath, you might find that you are extra receptive to stimuli. Telepaths generally have extrasensory perception. This means that their senses are extra sharp, compared to that of an average person. Going through a telepathic awakening heightens your senses, especially your sense of hearing. When you start seeing colors of light just outside your peripheral vision, you may be going through an awakening. If you are extra receptive to sensory input, you might find that you can sense others' thoughts and feelings before they even voice them. For instance, you may find yourself completing other people's sentences for them, and not just occasionally; it happens every time. And this does not happen with only the people you know; it happens with different individuals. This is associated with telepathy as a psychic gift.

5. You are Highly Empathic

This is related to the above sign but in a different way. Empathy is the ability to put yourself in the shoes of another person. Telepaths can do this because of their ability to sense people's thoughts and feelings. When you can find out the reasons behind a person's thoughts and emotions, it is much easier to empathize with them. If you are the type who feels the emotions of others strongly, even if they are nowhere near you, then you are most likely a telepath. You are also an empath. Being highly empathic is an indication of your hyper-awareness.

6. You Regularly Experience Different Sensations

If you often experience a tingling sensation in the area between your brows, that is another sign that you might be a telepath. The area between your brows is the home of your third-eye chakra. The third-eye chakra is instrumental to your telepathic ability. In fact, without the third eye, a lot of psychic abilities would simply be impossible. You cannot see beyond your physical sight without the third eye. The third eye makes it possible to see and sense things that the physical eyes cannot see. The third-eye area usually starts tingling more frequently when the third-eye chakra is opening up or when you are receiving specific energy signals. The tingling may be more frequent during the opening and developmental stage when your chakra is developing. Generally, it is harmless and usually goes away after a while. Pay attention to the third-eye area and watch out for tingling or any other similar sensation. A simple meditative session can help you calm the sensation when it starts.

7. You Feel a Stronger Connection to the Spirit World

Being telepathic makes you develop a link to the spiritual realms. As a result, you may sense the presence of spirits in the physical world more quickly than others. Your connection to the spirit world surges the more you become aware of your gift, so, don't be surprised. You may find that you can connect to the spirit world to interact with your loved ones or other people's loved ones. It is not uncommon for people with telepathic gifts to eventually become mediums. It seems to be a natural progression when the awakening happens.

8. You Feel Inclined to Spirituality

Many spiritualists don't just start out being interested in spiritualism or psychical abilities. More often than not, they turn to spiritualism when they become more aware of their gifts. If you are reading this book right now, it is probably because you think you are a telepath, and you probably are. One thing about telepathic awakening is that it usually pushes people towards learning. If you are a telepath, you undoubtedly feel the urge to learn more about the gift. As your awakening happens and you start getting rid of your old skin, your desire to become more spiritually developed surges. This pushes you to work more on spiritual transformation, growth, and evolution.

9. You Receive Intuitive Hits More Regularly

Intuitive hits can come in different ways. You might be the type to receive visions through your third eye, or maybe you just sense when something is about to happen. Regardless, both are signs of strong intuitive abilities. Depending on who you are, you may find this frightening or exciting. Fortunately, you can take steps to minimize the rate at which you receive hits if they frighten you. However, doing this means that you are preventing yourself from experiencing a full telepathic awakening. You should embrace your abilities and use them to help others.

10. You Get Headaches More Frequently

Headaches are awful, but you can't keep them away when going through a telepathic awakening. These headaches are caused by the opening of your third-eye chakra and the resulting influx of energy. The best way to control the headaches is to soak your feet in water, preferably lukewarm water. Doing this grounds the energy you are receiving, meaning it is carried away from your head. Consider adding Epsom salt to the water as it makes it more relaxing for you.

The first time you experience your telepathic gift, it may feel strange and unfamiliar to you. But this shouldn't be a reason for you to fret. The feelings you experience during your awakening are entirely normal; every telepath experiences these things. You shouldn't be frightened. As a matter of fact, you should be excited because you now have a window for spiritual growth and evolution. So, be excited about the new journey. Make sure you become more aware of yourself and your environment. If any of the points discussed above feel familiar to you, the next best step you can take is nurturing your telepathic gift.

Chapter Five: Enhancing Your Spiritual Energy Levels

To start unlocking your telepathic gift, you must first understand which psychic sense(s) you are working with. As a beginner to the practice of telepathy, you cannot navigate the psychic world effectively unless you master all the psychic senses and find out which ones you are more in tune with. It's just like when you are an infant, and you are just getting to know the world; you have to master your five physical senses first. Until you become familiar with all the psychic senses, you may not connect the experiences you have had to any psychic concept. When you are unaware of what you are working with, you simply can't find the right word or terms to define your experiences. But once you learn these things, your experiences become definable and real to you in a way that aligns with your abilities.

Learning and mastering the psychic senses can empower you, especially as a new psychic who is just becoming familiar with the psychic world. More importantly, you need the knowledge to determine where you fall in the spectrum of the psychic senses. By learning, you understand what is natural to you and what you actually need to improve and enhance. Knowledge of the psychic senses will reduce the spirit world's seeming detachment from the "real" world. It may also make psychic gifts appear less mysterious to you. So, introducing you to the "Clair" senses.

I have mentioned things, such as clairvoyance, clairsentience, clairaudience, etc., in previous chapters. I have also talked about how important they are to developing your abilities as a telepath. These three are part of what makes up your psychic senses. The psychic senses are also called the Clairs, the para senses, meta senses, or soul senses.

In your physical human body, you use your eyes to see, your nose to smell, your skin to feel, your tongue to taste, and your ears to hear. But when it comes to the Clair senses, you can experience all of these sensations but not through your physical senses. This means that you can see without using your naked human eyes. You have more psychic senses than physical senses. However, attaching the psychic senses to your ordinary five senses makes it easier for you to understand. After all, the psychic senses also perform the functions of your physical senses. The only difference is that these senses allow you to sense things that are beyond the physical world.

One thing shared by all the psychic senses is that they all begin with "Clair," the French word for clear. Basically, when you see Clair in front of any of the psychic senses, it means that sense is amplified and made clearer. Naturally, we all have all the psychic senses. But according to experts, we are dominant in at least one or two of these senses. This means, even though you have all the Clair senses, some are more prominent for you than others. You may be able to use one Clair sense naturally and effortlessly, which means it is your dominant psychic sense. However, you will need practice to develop and sharpen all the other senses. Also, you can control when you use these senses. After all, if you are clairvoyant, you don't want to start seeing spirits everywhere you go without being able to make them go away. Naturally, one of your goals should be to learn how to control when you tap into your psychic senses. Below are the psychic "Clair" senses to help you determine which one is your dominant sense. You should be able to tell from the definition of the terms and the traits that come with each sense.

Clairvoyance

Clairvoyance simply means "clear seeing." It is the psychic sense that allows you to see energy. Basically, clairvoyance is psychic seeing. Clairvoyants, through their third eye, can see things beyond the ordinary; things that the average human eyes cannot see. They also see visions. Clairvoyance is one of the more popular senses. Even if you have never dabbled in anything psychic, chances are you have already heard that word before. Using your clairvoyance sense, you can see beyond time and space. This means that you can see the astral world, the spirits, the future, and many other things that your human eyes simply cannot see. Clairvoyance tends to be the dominant sense in very visual people. Being visual means that you understand concepts and ideas best when presented to you in a form that requires you to use your eyes, such as a piece of writing, a picture, or even a drawing.

Clairvoyance is the intuitive sixth sense that you have likely heard people talk about before. This sense works with your mind's eye, which is also your third eye or spiritual eyes. People with clairvoyance as their dominant sense can see energy in different forms, including light, colors, images, pictures, and movements. Often, when some people hear the word "psychic," the only thing that comes to mind is clairvoyance. However, there is a slight difference between the two. Clairvoyance isn't the only thing it takes to be psychic. When someone says they are psychic, it doesn't automatically mean that they are clairvoyant; they may be clairsentient or claircognizant. Psychic is a broad term, and clairvoyance happens to fall under that term.

Often, clairvoyants receive their spiritual messages in the form of a screen that contains symbols and pictures. Or it may be the visual outline of a person with specific traits. It may also come up as a warning of something that will happen in the future. You can tell their unique individual characteristics when you see a person because it will appear visually. You may also be able to see something that will happen in the future. It doesn't matter if the message appears on a screen or not, though. As long as you receive your messages in the form of visuals, your dominant psychic sense is clairvoyance. Psychic mediums who see visions and receive messages from the spirit worlds are typically spiritual telepaths. They can communicate with the spirit world through their mind's eye.

As a telepath, if your dominant psychic sense is clairvoyance, it means that you will be very good at mental impressing, which is the ability to telepathically plant visual information in people's minds.

Clairsentience

Clairsentience literally means "clear feeling." It is the psychic ability to feel the energy. If you are the type of person who enters a room and becomes immediately bombarded with the different energies in the room, as you can just feel them, then you are clairsentient. If you can sense what another person is thinking or feeling, this is another possible sign. Clairsentients are highly sensitive people because they "feel" energy instead of seeing or hearing it. You may also refer to clairsentience as "gut feeling." When you meet a new person and immediately feel relaxed with them, your clairsentience sense is at work; when you meet someone and they "feel" off to you, that is also your clairsentient sense.

A clairsentient is a person with the ability to feel what is hidden from the physical senses. As someone whose dominant psychic sense is clairsentience, you can feel positive and negative emotions from people and spirits, as well as everything that has energy coursing through them in the cosmos. Everything in the world is made up of energy. Most people cannot see the energy, but it is always radiating around every one of us at all times. When you "feel" a kind of way about another individual, that is their energy you are feeling. Just like clairvoyants can see energy, clairsentients can feel the energy. Being clairsentient means that you can feel the energy with accuracy. In other words, you can accurately decipher what it is you are feeling from another person. Everyone is born to feel the energy, but not everyone has clairsentience as their dominant psychic sense. An intriguing thing about being clairsentient is that you don't just sense what is happening in the present; you can also feel the past and future emotional states of others. This means that you may be able to sense their future. Like all the other psychic senses, clairsentience is also associated with the sixth sense, your sense of intuition.

Clairsentients are affected by different influences. However, it all boils down to sensitivity. They are highly sensitive to changes in energy around them, no matter how subtle. Having clairsentience as your dominant sense means that you can feel inner and outer energy in ways that others cannot, even when they do have that sense too. The energy you feel ranges from feelings to spiritual objects, perceptions, and the future.

If you are clairsentient, you may be able to telepathically communicate through feelings. For example, clairsentient telepaths tend to feel when someone is in danger, regardless of their distance.

Note: Clairsentients are often confused for empaths, but there is a slight difference between the two. Empaths are people who are highly sensitive to the feelings and emotions of others. Clairsentients tend to be empaths because they are also sensitive to feelings. However, clairsentients are different because they feel energy across the universe, not just from their environment.

Claircognizance

Claircognizance is clear knowing. This is the psychic sense dominant in people who learn about people, events, and other things psychically. Claircognizants just know things. If you have ever wondered how you just happen to know things about others for no reason, you are cognizant. The knowledge comes from the spirits, but you cannot know this when you aren't spiritually inclined. You simply spend your time wondering how you know things. Claircognizance is an impressive psychic sense because things literally just fall out of nowhere into your mind. You have no practical explanation for where these things are from and why they are coming to you specifically.

Let's say you are headed home from work. You have the regular route that you pass every day. There is another route, but you never use that route. On this fortunate day, for no reason, you just decide that you will follow the route you never use. Even your coworker is surprised, and they try to convince you to just follow the regular route you always go through. But something just tells you to go through the second route; so, off you go. The second route is longer than the first one, making you get home 5 minutes later than you usually would. On getting home, you settle on the couch and turn on the TV. What do you find on the TV? A news broadcast about a blockade on your regular route. People are stuck in traffic, and it doesn't seem like it would be clearing anytime soon. Amazed, you chuckle and thank your luck for helping you.

Well, that is less of your luck and more of your cognizance sense. Even though you don't consciously realize it, your spirit guide dropped knowledge about the blockade in your mind. That is why you decided to leave your usual route for the second one.

If people always come to you when they have a problem, this may signify that you are claircognizant. People come to you because they believe you'd "know" the solution. As a claircognizant person, you have the gift to immediately tell a fake person from a real one. You don't even have to feel a way about them; you just know. How do you tell if claircognizance is your dominant psychic sense? It's easy; pay attention and see if information appears in your head out of nowhere. Also, see how you feel about the information you receive. If your heart is true and real to them, you might be claircognizant. The significant difference between clairvoyants and claircognizants is whereas clairvoyants see things, claircognizants know things. They don't need to see something before they know it.

Claircognizance is one of the vital psychic senses that you need to utilize your telepathy gift.

Clairaudience

Clairaudience is the fourth psychic sense, and it literally translates to "clear hearing." This is one sense that you really have to develop if you want to use your telepathic abilities. It does not matter whether it is your dominant psychic sense or not. If you are clairaudient, it means that you can hear things beyond the physical or normal range. You intuitively receive information and guidance from spirits and other beings outside of the material realm via hearing. This does not mean that you only hear things that are happening in the spiritual realms, though. What it means is that you can hear things that the ordinary five senses cannot pick up. For instance, you can hear another person's thoughts as clearly as if they were speaking out loud. If you aren't psychically aware, you might even feel like you are going crazy. The very thought of this can be frightening, which is why it helps to be psychically aware.

If you are clairaudient, the information will come to you in a variety of ways. For one, the information might come as unintelligible sounds. The sounds may be names, phrases, words, and even lyrics of music. When your clairaudient sense is awakening, you will experience a range of sensations from ringing or buzzing in your ears to pressure on your ears. Eventually, you may start hearing voices in your head. Naturally, the voices you hear will be different from the ones that you usually hear. It may sound as if another person is speaking directly into your head from beside you. Or it may sound like an echo from another dimensional plane. Don't be surprised if the voice also sounds like that of a loved one who is no longer with you on earth.

Many people are born to be clairaudient, which means that clairaudience is typically their dominant psychic ability. However, even if you aren't born as a clairaudient, you can acquire the skill through practice and consistency. Note that clairaudient messages can be received in four different ways. The first way is through your own very voice. This form of the message is subtle, and you may appear to be having a dialogue in your mind. But really, the voice you are hearing is that of your spirit guide or any other spirit. This is different from the inner guidance you receive when you are attuned with your higher self. You have to learn how to differentiate between the inner guidance and the voice of clairaudience.

The second way clairaudient messages are received is through spirit voices. Remember that these are all forms of telepathic communication. If you aren't receiving messages telepathically through your own voice, you may be receiving through the voices of the spirits. These usually sound like the voices of loved ones and acquaintances that have passed away. You will hear it exactly as it was when they were present with you on earth. Another way you may receive clairaudient messages is through sounds. For instance, you may hear your name when you are alone. You can also hear noises, whispering, talking, or the sound of the radio. The critical thing to note here is that the sound you hear will make sense to you. If you can't find the source of the noise physically, the message may be generated by a spirit nearby. Finally, clairaudient messages sometimes come as warnings. In cases of distress, you may hear a message out loud even when no one around you has said anything.

This may be anything from ringing to yelling. Pay attention to things such as these.

Besides these four senses, which are considered the primary psychic senses, there are two other senses you should pay attention to.

Clairalience

Clairalience is a sense of clear smelling. It is when you can smell odors that have no physical presence. For example, when someone is near you, one of the things you smell from them could be the scent of their perfume. However, if you have the gift of clairalience, you will be able to smell their perfume even when they are nowhere around you. You will also be able to smell it when none of their possessions, such as clothes, is with you. When you smell something from someone you know in their absence, it means that their energy is actually around you. Whatever you smell is from the energy in your environment. If your dominant psychic ability is clairalience, your sense of smell can be compelling and overwhelming. A strong and powerful sense of smell may connect you to past or future events or memories. Usually, the odor or fragrance you smell is from the spirit world. It suggests that the spirit is trying to communicate with you. The smell may be related to the spirit. For instance, you may smell a person's favorite tobacco when they were alive. Or, as I said before, it may be their perfume.

While clairalience isn't mainly a sense you require to be a telepath, it can definitely come in handy.

Clairgustance

Clairgustance is a sense of clear tasting. It refers to the ability to taste things that aren't really in the physical realm with you. Spirits can transmit messages in the form of flavors. Usually, the flavor will be something they loved while they were alive in the physical world. Your clairgustance sense may come to you as a surprise because the accompanying experience usually is sudden and out-of-the-blue. Sometimes, it comes when a deceased relative attempts to trigger a memory of an event or any other thing associated with a specific food or flavor that was once their favorite food. Or it could be your own favorite food that they used to make for you. There was a time

I simply used to taste banana in my mouth even when I hadn't had a banana in a while. You may have experienced this before, as it is quite a common occurrence.

Now that you know all the six psychic senses, the next step is to identify your dominant psychic sense to learn how this will help you will your telepathic awakening. Usually, most people's dominant psychic sense is either clairvoyance, clairsentience, claircognizance, or clairaudience. Clairgustance and clairalience tend to be complimentary psychic senses. The simple exercise below will help you recognize your dominant psychic sense.

- Sit in a comfortable room with no distractions.

- Begin scanning the length and breadth of the room. Ensure you pay attention to all the details in the room, no matter how trivial the detail appears to be. More importantly, note the sounds, sights, and scents in the space.

- Now, gently close your eyes. Focus on the in and out of your breath. Make your breaths slow and deep as you try to review the things you noticed while scanning the room. Did something, in particular, stand out to you because of its appearance? Was it the sound of something that stood out? Did any strong feeling register in your tummy as you scanned?

- Pay attention to how you feel about the energies in the space.

- This little exercise is called an environmental scan. It can help you ascertain which of the Clair senses we have just discussed is your dominant psychic sense. You shouldn't practice this exercise in just one place. Ensure you do it in different areas, from the park to the bar to your workplace and even the subway. The more aware you are of your immediate surrounding, the easier it will be to notice shifts in energy around you. You will also be able to find out whether you see, feel, hear, or just know that there has been a shift in the energy around you. As you read on, you will learn how to unlock your dominant psychic skill for telepathy practices.

Chapter Six: Using Meditation to Open Up

One of the things that have been made clear right from the beginning of this book is that telepathy cannot occur in a chaotic mind. After all, how are you supposed to send or receive telepathic messages if your mind is in a constant state of chatter and noise? Telepathic messages can only be received when you've trained your mind to always remain in a state of calm and quiet, regardless of where you are or what you are doing. Using your psychic skills requires you to be present in the moment. Without being present, there is no way you can notice or observe the shifts in energies around you. Mindfulness is a vital part of using your psychic gifts.

As you should already know, meditation is the number one tool for calming the mind. Whether you want to learn how to see energy, read energy, or communicate with the spiritual realms, you cannot do all these unless you make meditation a consistent part of your routine. To awaken your psychic senses and the spiritual part of yourself, you need to understand the power of meditation. The first step to using your psychic senses is to become in tune with your inner self. Communicating with your inner self or your higher self is the first practice you will have in developing your telepathy. The more in tune you are with yourself, the more your psychic senses open up, and the clearer your gift of telepathy becomes to you. Therefore, meditation is a vital part of the steps you need to awaken your dormant powers.

There are different types of meditation. However, you only need two to open up your psychic senses. The first is spiritual meditation, which you may also call transcendental meditation. The second is chakra meditation. If you remember, I said that the chakras are your body's energy system. The third-eye chakra, which is the sixth sense connected to all psychic abilities, is part of the chakra system. Unless the chakras are balanced, aligned, and in a healthy state, it would be impossible to use your psychic senses or your telepathy gift. Even if the third-eye chakra is in an excellent state, other chakras can still affect your ability to send and receive telepathic messages. This is precisely why you must learn how to use chakra meditation to keep your chakras open to the flow of vital energy at all times. Unless energy is flowing through your chakras as it should, your physical body will be in a state of unrest and illness.

Spiritual Meditation

If you have never tried spiritual meditation before, it can be challenging to understand just how helpful meditation can be in developing your psychic senses. In the chapter where I talked about the benefits of using your telepathy gift, I mentioned many benefits directly tied to meditation. You should never forget about meditation because it is all about becoming intimately aware of yourself. As I have said, becoming aware of yourself is one step you must take towards awakening your psychic senses.

Spiritual meditation is a wholesome experience that unravels the very depth of who you are. This form of meditation strips away all the misinformed perceptions you may have about yourself to show you your real self. Spiritual meditation opens you up to your true self, whom you may have been hiding from. For instance, if you have always suspected that you have psychic abilities but have been shying away out of fear or anything else, meditation can help you see yourself for who you really are. This will allow you to stop running from your abilities and gifts. Spiritual meditation grounds you in the present, which is precisely where you need to be if you want to attune to the energies around you. Naturally, you may be wondering what exactly you have to gain from meditation. Well, there are several things to gain, and all will prove helpful in your telepathic journey.

The biggest gain from meditation is probably the fact that it unplugs you from the material world's frenetic energy. When you meditate, you are slowing down and detaching yourself from all the franticness of the world you live in. This helps you focus on what's within you, opening up your path to perception. When this happens, you get to know yourself and the "you" within yourself awakens. You become more aware of the present, and you let go of thoughts of the past and the future. You ground yourself in the present moment.

As humans, the root of our worldly suffering is the belief that we are a distinct entity from the Creator and the people around us. Contrary to what you may believe, you are not merely a composition of body, mind, feelings, and memories. You are much more than that. However, this false belief becomes ingrained in our unconscious mind, creating pain with it. Meditation helps you to become aware of this damaging belief so that you can let it go. If you don't let it go, the pain can obstruct you from unlocking your powers and abilities, all of which come from the connection you share with your Creator. Meditation awakens your inherent desire to understand and embrace the truth of your being. You become willing to accept the gifts you have. Acceptance is crucial to using your telepathy skills. Without acceptance, you are unconsciously blocking yourself from attaining a level that has been naturally bestowed on you.

Below, I have some spiritual meditation practices that you can incorporate into your daily routine to awaken your true self, and in the process, your psychic senses. You can do these exercises individually or combine them if that is what you want. The best way to use these meditation exercises is to begin with the breathing meditation exercise and then follow it up with the other exercises. Take it slowly and add the exercises to your routine one by one. You can meditate at any time of the day. I do my meditations upon waking up every morning and before I retire to bed every evening. I recommend that you follow this schedule too. Then, you can practice any other time of the day if you feel the urge. The more comfortable you become with meditation, the easier you will find it to meditate every day.

Before you begin daily meditation, I suggest that you set up a meditation space in one part of your home. This space should be in the quietest part of your home, somewhere you are less likely to be interrupted and distracted. Whenever you have to meditate, ensure that your eyes are alone and your mobile gadgets are all turned off. This will help you keep technological distractions away. Also, your eyes must be closed for all of the meditation exercises. You may start meditation with just 5 to 10 minutes sessions every day. So, you do your meditations for 5 to 10 minutes in the morning and then another 5 to 10 minutes in the evening. Gradually, you can build up the duration of your meditation exercises to 30 minutes. Don't be afraid to build up to 60 minutes if you can. The more you focus on tuning in with the light within you, the more it will reflect in your physical life. More importantly, the more heightened your psychic senses will be.

Basic Breathing Meditation

As the name implies, this is an essential meditation exercise that can get you started on the journey to unlocking your psychic senses. But don't let the seeming simplicity of the breathing meditation delude you into underestimating its power and effectiveness. This meditation is all about paying attention to your breath. Simple, right? Well, it is simple, but it can also be incredibly hard to master. The mind is a very distracting organ. As you try to focus on your breathing, your thoughts will try to take you away from the present. When you focus on your breath, you are removing yourself from the physical world and bringing yourself to focus on what is inside you. Gradually, your mind will start to calm and settle. As your ego-mind withdraws, you become open to a deeper part of yourself. Awareness begins to unfold. On just the surface level, basic breathing meditation is quite powerful. It can facilitate healing for your physical body. The best way to do this exercise is to focus on your breath without changing how you breathe. By doing this, you accept yourself and give yourself a chance to be just as you are. The longer this meditation is, the calmer your mind becomes. When your mind reaches a certain level of calm, your psychic senses become more alert and heightened. At that moment, sending and receiving a telepathic message becomes very easy and quick. How do you do the basic breathing meditation?

- Go to your meditation place and assume a comfortable sitting position on the ground or chair. It doesn't matter which one you use, but I recommend using the ground as a beginner. Eventually, you will be able to meditate even while you are standing or in any place at all. However, if you are new to meditation, it is best to practice in a space where there will be little to no distractions.

- Close your eyes gently. Pay attention to your sitting position and see if any part of you feels uncomfortable. Adjust your body until you are entirely confident that you are comfortable.

- Now, bring your attention to your breathing. Focus on the rhythm of your breathing. Do not attempt to change the way you are breathing. For instance, don't try to make your breathing slower. Even if you don't do this, your breathing will later slow down and become more profound.

- Do not take your focus away from your breathing. Let it remain as it is. Even if it shifts, remain focused. Let your body breathe precisely as it wants to. The only thing you are required to do is focus on your breathing. Notice as you inhale and exhale. Be with your breath.

- Naturally, you will find your thoughts wandering off as you focus on your breathing. Every time this happens, gently call your attention back to the present with no judgment.

- When you first begin this meditation, you may notice that your mind continually shifts away from breathing. Don't blame yourself for this. It is a very normal part of the process. Just bring your attention back every time it drifts away. Over time, you will be able to meditate without having your mind drift off so frequently. The more practice you put in, the better you will become at calming your mind to receive psychic messages.

Mindfulness Meditation

The purpose of mindfulness meditation is to help you realize the importance of the present. This meditation helps you learn that time is an illusion that exists to distract you from the present. The present is the most important thing to focus on at any point in time. When you focus on the moment, you let go of your ego – the one thing keeping you from actualizing your full potentials. Mindfulness meditation teaches you to focus on the NOW. Essentially, this is what you need to master if you want to experience your true self as it is. This meditation stills the chatter and noises of your mind so that you can gain access to your deeper consciousness. The telepathic spiritual message often comes in different forms when one is focused on the present and not the past or the future. Being present in the moment is the key to accessing reality.

- Start mindfulness meditation by first practicing the simple breathing exercise detailed above. Let go of all the thoughts, fears, and worries that may hold you back from accessing your deeper consciousness. Forget everything you think you know and focus on the things you are trying to know.

- Imagine a table in front of you. Imagine yourself putting all of your fears, concerns, worries, and burdens on this table. Cast them on the table one by one.

- Take a vacation from all your perceptions of yourself, as well as other people's perception of you. Let go of the person you think yourself to be, the person you want yourself to be, and the person other people think you are. Let it all go and feel yourself become free and light.

- Now, focus on the moment. Pay attention to the sensations in your body. Notice any sound, smell, and everything else your senses are picking up in your environment.

- Every time a concern or thought comes to mind during your meditation, put it on the table before you.

- Allow yourself to sink deep into yourself; go past the surface chatter in your mind. Observe your thoughts as they float around in your mind but don't try to get involved with them. Just let them float.

While in this meditative state, you may feel a strain, as if you expect something to happen. Let this go as well and let your attention remain on the present. Be still, aware, and open to any psychic experience that may happen at that moment.

Remember that the purpose of these meditation exercises is not to use telepathy. The purpose is to help you open up your psychic senses so that you can use your gift. Unless the senses are open, this would be impossible.

Chakra Meditation

I have seen many supposed psychics say that you don't need to train your chakras to send and receive telepathic messages. This may appear valid to someone who has no knowledge of how psychic gifts work. Of course, the third-eye chakra is the chakra tied to psychic abilities from clairvoyance to clairaudience. Essentially, the third-eye chakra is the most important chakra for the use of psychic gifts. However, the third-eye chakra is part of a vital energy system. Even if you open your third-eye chakra, you will not be able to use your psychic senses as long as the other chakras are closed, blocked, or unaligned with the third-eye chakra. To successfully use your telepathy skill, you need to ensure that all your seven chakras are in a state of alignment. Plus, if you remember clearly, the solar plexus chakra is partly responsible for instinctual telepathy. The third-eye chakra makes mental telepathy and its four activities possible. Spiritual telepathy cannot be possible unless your crown chakra is awakened and aligned with the rest of the chakras. Therefore the chakra system as a whole has a crucial role to play in your ability to actualize your full psychic potential. Basically, we have seven chakras that make up your energy centers:

- The Root Chakra
- Sacral Chakra
- Solar Plexus Chakra
- Heart Chakra
- Throat Chakra
- Third-Eye Chakra

- Crown chakra

These seven chakras must always remain in a balanced and aligned state for your spiritual awakening to take place and your telepathic gift to unlock. More importantly, they must also be open to the flow of vital energy at all times. This is especially important to keep your physical, emotional, and spiritual body in the utmost health.

Below is a simple meditation exercise to open, balance, and align your seven chakras to enhance your psychic experiences. This should be done in the meditation space that we previously talked about.

- Sit in a comfortable position in your meditation space. Sit with your spine in an upright position without feeling rigid. Focus on your body, starting from the feet and working your way up. Pay attention to the sensation in each part of your body as you focus and feel the tension melt away.

- Next, focus on your breath. Gently pay attention as you inhale and exhale. You will notice that your breathing will become deeper and steadier. Picture the oxygen going into your lungs, traveling to every part of your body, from cell to organ to muscle.

- Now, visualize the beating of your heart and your heart chakra with it. Focus on the harmony in your body. Observe as all the parts come together to work as one. Pay attention to how your breath is giving life to every part of your body.

- It is time to bring attention to each of your seven chakras one by one. The point is to influx energy into each chakra as you focus on it. Begin with your root chakra, which is in the base of your spine. Visualize a body of energy swirling in a clockwise way and feel as the energy going in and out of your breath feeds this body of energy and makes it bigger and brighter.

- From the root chakra, move to your sacral chakra and do the same thing. Do this one at a time, from the sacral to the solar plexus chakra, until energy fills each chakra. Infuse each chakra with your life force energy. Note that it doesn't matter how much time you spend doing this. Take as much time as you need.

- The best way to do this is to work from the bottom to the highest chakra. Don't do the meditation the other way around, as this can result in an adverse effect.

- Once you have worked your way up to the highest chakra, your crown chakra, the final step is to visualize all your seven chakras getting fed by the ball of energy. As you do this, the chakras should come together to become more prominent, brighter, healthier, and more transparent. They should be supercharged and filled with energy.

Finally, open your eyes and remain in your meditation position for a while until you feel relaxed to move. Notice how your body feels newly refreshed and revitalized. At that very moment, your psychic senses will be all open and alert. Do the chakra meditation for 15 to 30 minutes any time you feel like your chakras are blocked and hindering your psychic senses. You will feel uplifted every time.

As you become more advanced in your spiritual and psychic journey, you will be exposed to more advanced forms of meditation that will enhance your abilities even more. Regardless of whether you are doing a basic or advanced meditation, there are some key things that you must have in your mind at all times.

First, the position is just as important as meditation itself. A comfortable position is a crucial part of any meditation, no matter the type of meditation. One of the best ways to ensure you are in the most comfortable position for your meditation is to stay away from the noise as much as possible. If possible, you should surround yourself with the greenery of nature. If your sitting position isn't comfortable, it would be difficult, maybe even impossible, to achieve your meditation goal, which is to calm and quieten your mind. However, your position shouldn't be so comfortable to where you can easily drift off to sleep. One of the best positions is to sit upright on a chair. If you are comfortable withstanding, you can stand with your back against the wall. The bottom line is that you must choose a position that works for you.

Second, when you meditate, you must immerse yourself in the process. Typically, when you have a task to complete, you plan the process and then execute it step by step. This is how we all complete our tasks. However, you should never do this with meditation because it shouldn't feel like a task. Meditation is something you should enjoy doing. Treating it like a task isn't ideal. Even though there are steps to follow, you must still allow everything to feel natural. Let the meditation take its course in an organic manner. Do not try to control the ambiance or the process. Be passive and let the process take charge. It should happen of its own accord. Don't be intent on getting it right or meeting a specific outcome. Again, let the meditation flow naturally.

Third, you must always acknowledge your floating thoughts when you are meditating. You cannot merely get rid of all your thoughts because you want to focus on your meditation. It does not work like that. When I say "let go" of your thought, this means you shouldn't bother engaging them, not ignore them completely. It is natural for your mind to be abuzz with all kinds of information while focusing on the present. The best way to deal with this is to accept those thoughts. No matter how hard you try not to, you will inevitably react to the thoughts.

To some extent, your thoughts will affect your concentration. The goal is not to respond to the thought; you must not allow your thoughts to dictate the meditation flow. This is where the challenge lies. Acknowledge your thoughts without responding to them. Let them drift away so you can refocus on your meditation.

As you sit there meditating, you may utter a prayer to the Divine. This doesn't necessarily have to be tied with any religion. Just choose a prayer and direct it to the Higher Being within yourself. The prayer can be anything you want or like. For instance, you can utter a prayer that goes like, "In the name of the Divine, I open myself up to the light, love, and the psychic doorway." This is a prayer that is targeted at helping you awaken your senses and your gifts quicker. You may also chant a mantra as you meditate. It all depends on what you want for yourself. Actually, saying a prayer as you breathe in and out can help you focus on your breathing and the present, which is the meditation's whole point.

Think of meditation as an opportunity for you to reflect on yourself. Tune in to your physical body and the sensations going through it as you meditate. Be in tune with your awareness and your presence in your meditative space. Be conscious of the flow of energy in your environment. Notice how you feel throughout the meditation. Your body will feel lighter; pay attention to the lightness. Accept your body's reaction to meditation.

Keep in mind that these meditation exercises' primary benefit is helping you calm your thoughts and emotions. In other words, the point is to get rid of the mental chatter, open up your psychic portals, and prepare yourself for a telepathic experience. Meditation will help you connect with your higher consciousness to tune in to the cosmos and everything within it.

Chapter Seven: Opening Your Third Eye

The third eye is the doorway to higher consciousness, the place where you gain the ability to see into other's souls, as well as your own. All the psychic skills we talked about in Chapter Five originate from intuition. The third-eye chakra is the seat of intuition. Without the third eye, there would be nothing like intuition or psychic gifts. Unless you open your third eye, you cannot unlock your telepathy. Opening your third eye means you have attained a level of enlightenment above any other you know. You may also call the third eye the inner eye or the Ajna. In Hindu tradition, they call the third eye the "eye of knowledge," which is the perfect way to sum up the third eye's function or ability. Any knowledge you receive via your clairvoyance, clairsentience, clairaudience, and claircognizance senses comes through your third eye because it is the pathway to enlightenment.

Opening the third eye isn't something you do once. It is a process that requires consistent meditation. When you start trying to open your third-eye chakra, it may feel like it is opening first. You may start to get the familiar sensations in the location of your third eye. And then, the sensations all vanish suddenly and may not come back until months later. This can be discouraging, but if you are truly ready, you will be able to exercise patience until the third eye opens up again. The process is usually full of trials and errors, which you must be mentally prepared for. But it doesn't happen until you are ready. So, if you don't think you are ready for the awakening of your third-eye chakra, you shouldn't bother with the process at all. If you open your third eye without ensuring that you are ready for it, you may experience different adverse effects.

As you already know, your third eye is located in the area between your eyebrows, although slightly higher. Basically, your third eye is on your forehead. That central point between your eyebrows is the seat of your inner wisdom, imagination, and intuition. Naturally, you cannot physically observe the third eye as you would your physical eyes. However, you can envision it using a visualization exercise.

Your third eye, as you can probably tell from the name, is responsible for:

- How you form gut feelings and experience instincts
- Your ability to see the bigger picture in life
- Creating a balance between emotion and logic

Therefore, when the third eye is open, you can use your intuition and inner wisdom to perceive and understand the things that defy logic. There is a profound difference in how you feel when your third eye is open and how you feel when it is closed.

Opening the third eye is incredible, but it also comes with many side effects that most people fail to consider. Before you start working on opening your third eye, you should understand the side effects and how best to handle them when they start pouring in. Awakening your third eye comes with many uncomfortable experiences that can turn you off the process if you aren't prepared for them. Going into the process without being prepared may result in you opting to close your third eye forever, and that is not something I want for you. As I have said, we all have a third eye. But just because everyone has a third eye does not mean we will experience the third eye's awakening in the same way. The sensations are more intense for some people than others. The point is to give you forewarning for the experience and outline techniques you can use to ensure your third eye is a source of enlightenment instead of distress.

Interestingly, some people have already awakened their third eye without realizing it. Innocently, they work on third eye exercises, trying to awaken an already opened third eye. Usually this happens because they have repressed their awareness of the awakening out of fear. If you have real gut feelings all the time, your third eye may already be wholly or partly open. No matter how you try to suppress your third eye, you will still get intuitive messages and gut feelings as long as it remains open. The more you get "baseless" intuitive messages that turn up accurate, the higher the possibility of your third eye being open already.

Apart from the fact that opening your third eye causes intense and powerful gut feelings, it results in several other side effects that are not physically comfortable. Here are some side effects to watch out for when you start working on opening your third eye.

- A mild feeling of pressure in your forehead, specifically the area between your eyebrows. This sensation may be similar to the sensation you would get if someone gently presses their finger between your eyebrows.

- You get visuals in your mind or dream about things right before that happens.

- Your environment seems sharper, and you sense brighter colors. The third eye allows you to assimilate details that you would ordinarily miss with your routine human eyes. The sharp environment can be overwhelming and intense when the third eye opens.

- Frequent headaches that could almost count as migraines, depending on how intense the awakening is. The headache may feel like you have a band wrapped around your head or pressure on your temple. This often happens due to your psychic senses' opening, which makes your mind sharper than ever.

Opening your third eye may seem complicated and almost impossible if your chakras or the third-eye chakra is blocked. You may also struggle due to an imbalance of the chakras, which is why I talked about chakra meditation to help you keep your chakras open, balanced, and aligned. Unless you get rid of the blockages in your third eye chakra, you cannot access your powers to their full potentials. Blockage and imbalance in the chakra can be caused by stress, exhaustion, resistance to your gifts, anxiety, and repeated conflicts. Remember that the third-eye chakra can be overactive or underactive, so you must pay attention to the cues you receive. If your third eye is underactive, you may struggle to unlock your psychic senses or concentrate. You may also feel anxious and disconnected from the world and the people around you. But if your third eye chakra is overactive, you may feel foggy and out of tune with reality. The best thing is to have the third eye chakra in a state of balance where it is neither underactive nor overactive.

What will happen when you do open your third eye?

Naturally, everyone has different reasons they want to open their third eye. At the base of it all is the desire to unlock the pathway to higher consciousness and enlightenment. Here are some things to expect from opening your eyes. The experience can be overwhelming and intense, so don't forget to use meditation to make it easier.

• Intense Dreams and Nightmares

If you open your third eye without being ready or knowing what to expect, it will severely affect your sleep. You may have intense dreams and nightmares. If you don't get enough sleep, this will leave you feeling dehydrated and fatigued every morning. What makes this particularly intense is that you may keep seeing the images from your dream or nightmare in your head. This makes it difficult for you to concentrate on anything or even relax. When you have a disrupted sleep schedule, every other aspect of your daily life will be disrupted as well.

Meditating every night before you go to sleep can help you counter this side effect of opening your third eye. By meditating before sleep, you put your mind in a state of calm and balance that makes it less possible for your third eye to act erratically. Additionally, you can keep a dream journal to monitor whatever happens in your dream while you are asleep. The good thing about vivid dreams is that they never really go away at once. So, even when you wake up, you will still remember your dream as clearly as if you were still dreaming. Keeping a dream journal can help you decipher any reoccurring theme in your dreams and nightmares. If you process and understand the imagery and symbolism that appear in

---

your dreams, your third eye will automatically stop flooding you with the same thing every night. The important thing to never forget here is that there is always a message embedded in any vivid dreams you have. So, put in the work to uncover that message.

• Frighteningly Accurate Intuition

Forget gut feelings. When your third eye starts opening, you may become scared of yourself due to your intuitions' accuracy. When you have just opened your third eye, your gift will feel more like a burden to you. This is normal and understandable. You will become so good at predicting the future and others' behavior that you feel unnerved. You may feel daunted by the sheer accuracy of everything you see, and this may even prompt you to want to close your third eye. If you feel like this, remember why you started in the first place and bring your attention back to how your gift can help you and the people around you. Over time, you will become used to being accurate all the time, and you will no longer feel unnerved or daunted. Whatever happens, don't repress the intuitions you receive. You can reduce the intuitions' frequency by learning to open and close the psychic pathway at will. Trying to push them away or repress them might increase their frequency and intensity. Remind yourself why you chose to open your third eye and all the good things you can achieve by keeping it open. Never forget that it is the key to being more informed about your future.

• Fearlessness

Most people report developing a feeling of fearlessness after opening their third eye. Some say they feel almost invincible, like superman. If you feel this same way, know that it is very typical and expected. Opening your third eye is profoundly empowering and can result in a surge in your self-confidence. If you don't pay attention, though, the feeling of fearlessness can become unhealthy.

Contrary to what many people believe, fear is a necessary and essential emotion; it is crucial to your survival. First of all, understand that opening your third eye doesn't make you superman or superwoman; it doesn't make you invincible. Secondly, do not discard the rational or logical part of your mind because of your new-found enlightenment. Remember that the third eye is supposed to be the balance between logic and emotion. When necessary, ensure you engage the logical part of your third eye instead of relying entirely on intuition.

What happens when the third eye is overactive?

The result of having an overactive third eye is usually intense psychic and psychological distress. The third eye becomes overactive when there is an energy overdrive. As a result, you may feel as though you are lost in a sea of visions. You may be continuously bombarded with pieces of information with little or nothing to do with you and the people around you. If you don't ground yourself well enough, an overactive third eye can knock you off your feet.

One of the most common signs of an overactive third eye is an overindulgence of the fantasy world. Basically, one loses touch with reality and becomes obsessed with a fantasy world. Another obvious sign is a fear of the visions appearing and passing through one's mind's eye. When you open your third eye without getting support and balance from all the other chakras, your third eye may become overactive because of the energy influx.

The never-ending flow of thoughts and visions from an overactive third eye can be mentally overwhelming and exhausting. If you aren't careful, it may disrupt your life. Consequentially, you may find it challenging to make the simplest of decisions. This indecisiveness is the consequence of a lack of clarity, clouded judgment, absence of focus, and an inability to separate fantasy from reality. In this state, even when you receive psychic messages, you may not make sense of them. An overactive third eye will manifest in these ways:

- Headaches that never go away
- Seizures
- Inability to sleep
- Vision problems
- Nausea
- Sinus problems
- Hallucinations
- Anxiety
- Fogginess

- Lack of mental clarity

- Delusions and paranoia

Note that the point of discussing the effects of an overactive third eye is not to scare you; instead, I want you to be enlightened before you take the big step of opening your third eye. If the visions become insufferable, you can quickly slow them down. You can communicate with the source of the knowledge or guidance and humbly request more time to better yourself to receive all the information. If your visions are getting out of hand, then you should work on anchoring yourself to the Earth so that all the extra energies can go into the earth. Your spirit guide will also be willing to offer protection and guidance to make the experience more comfortable for you. Gently ask your spirit guide to send the information in ways that make it more comfortable to access, process, and understand.

Some ways to even out the energy in your third eye are to make positive and healthy lifestyle changes. Incorporate whole foods into your diet and exercise consistently. Other high vibrational practices that can help you balance the third-eye chakra's energy so it is neither overactive nor underactive include energy healing, Reiki healing, aromatherapy, etc.,

Now that you know everything to expect with the opening of the third eye chakra, let's get to how you can open your third eye!

There are several techniques you can use for awakening your third eye chakra. The first I want to talk about is the third-eye meditation.

Third-Eye Meditation

Meditation is basically to help you attune your consciousness or help you awaken your third eye. Still, the third-eye meditation is specifically different from other meditations we discussed in the previous chapter. While there are similarities in the meditation, the differences are much more important to pay attention to than the similarities. Everything I said about meditation from location to position applies to your third-eye meditation. So, refer back to the previous chapter if you need to.

- Begin with your breathing exercise, as breathing is the foundation for all types of meditation. Follow the instructions under the breathing meditation guidelines in chapter six.

- Empty your mind so you can focus on your third eye. Remember that your third eye is located in the center of your forehead. Below your eyelids, try moving your eyes upward to the location of your third eye. Let them remain there as you continue with your breathing exercise to maintain focus. Count backward from 100 to 1 as you focus. Don't be discouraged if you don't find your third eye instantly. Just focus on meditating and counting the numbers.

- Once you finish counting from 100 backward, you should be in the right state of mind to access your third eye. When you maintain your focus well enough, you will sense darkness everywhere, excluding the third eye. The light will be on, which suggests that your third eye is activating. Once your third eye becomes awakened and activated, you will observe that your brain is relaxed and functioning at a higher level than usual. The left and right hemispheres of your brain will be in sync, and you will be hyper-aware of the energy in your environment.

- If you feel energy coursing in and around your body, it means that you have awakened your third eye. If you can focus intensely on a visualized image without your mind getting distracted by anything else, this is another sign that your third eye is alive.

- Next, you have to allow yourself to experience the third eye. People react differently to the awakening of the third eye. You, like some people, may experience flashing visuals passing through your mind. The visuals may be images of people, nature, wildlife, and other scenes that you have likely seen before. People who have experienced this typically describe it as seeing one's thoughts as if they were being presented on a whiteboard.

- Remain focused on your third eye for at least 10 minutes. You may experience a mild headache the first time you try to awaken your third eye. Don't be scared – the more you practice, the fewer headaches you will experience. Try to visualize and focus on a specific image or object as you take in the experience. The point of this is to center your mind and help you stay in the moment.

- After 10 to 15 minutes, slowly call yourself out of your meditation. Take your focus away from your third eye back to your breath. Become aware of your breathing and focus on it as it goes in and out of your nostrils. You may count from 100 to 1 once again. Doing this will help you focus as you bring yourself out of meditation.

The third-eye activation may be slow or fast for you, depending on several factors. However, the timeframe doesn't really matter as long as you do it the right way. You can hasten the process of awakening your third eye by practicing the third-eye meditation every day. Daily practice makes activation much more accessible and possibly quicker. Don't forget to use mental focus to improve concentration and keep the mind's eye open. You may also practice some Hatha Yoga, which is very helpful with the seven chakras' balancing and alignment. As you practice your meditation, don't forget to remain in touch with your inner self. This should be the most critical aspect of your practice.

Sharpening Your Intuition

After opening your third eye with the meditation above, there are other ways to ensure that your third eye stays in great shape. Since the third eye is the intuition's seat, strengthening the third eye starts with sharpening your intuition.

I like to recommend to people to start by fostering silence of the mind. You may be thinking, "Oh, isn't that what meditation is all about?" Yes, meditation is all about helping your mind cultivate silence. But you cannot be meditating every minute of the day, especially if you have to work or go to school. So, your best option is to find other ways to cultivate silence of the mind. Fostering silence means readying your mind for psychic messages at any time. Telepathic messages don't tell you before they pop in, so you have to be ready to receive or send them at all times. If your mind hasn't learned to be silent, you will miss many crucial messages. You can foster silence by sitting in nature or taking a walk in a park or forest. You can also do it by absorbing yourself in your favorite sport or art. This brings me to how creativity can help you sharpen your intuition.

Nurturing your creative side can help develop and enhance your intuition. Open yourself up to creativity and let it flow through you freely. Let your imagination loose or immerse yourself in activities that require you to be creative. For example, learn a new art such as painting or sketching. As you practice this new craft, allow inspiration to flow from your third eye through your hands. You will be surprised at the results you achieve. Creativity loosens your rational mind. Your rational mind is part of what contributes to the mental chatter in your head. It is always there to comment on every step you take, right or wrong. It is that part of you that wants to control your actions to achieve a specific outcome. When you get creative, you are hushing this part of your mind and preventing it from dictating how reality should be to you. More importantly, you are opening yourself up to possibilities. By doing this, you are allowing your third eye to unravel and blossom.

Affirmations are great for targeting and replacing a negative belief system that could potentially impact your third eye. The purpose of third-eye affirmations is to replace negative beliefs with positive ones. They are instrumental in balancing your third-eye chakra and sharpening your intuitive senses. Third-eye affirmations should be created to focus on your guts, instincts, spirituality, and a sense of purpose. Here are some effective third-eye affirmations to help enhance your intuitive senses.

- "I open myself up to the guidance of my inner teacher."
- "I am aware of my intuitions. I hear them. I feel them. I sense them. I know they will guide me on my life purpose."
- "I will make the right decisions in life and do so very easily."
- "I believe in the guidance of my third eye."
- "I am intuitive, and I know what is right from wrong."

- "I am open to unlimited possibilities."

- "The guidance of my third eye will lead me to my purpose."

You can be as creative as you want with your affirmations. The point is to make sure they are all positive and geared towards developing and enhancing your intuition.

The color of the third-eye chakra is purple. You can get purple energy stones and jewelry to keep your third-eye chakra open and heal it when necessary. Any time your chakra feels like it is blocked, simply wear your jewelry with purple energy stones. Or you can get large energy crystals and keep them in your pocket, home, or office. Whenever you need to heal or unblock your third-eye chakra, pick up the crystal., gently squeeze, and focus on it for some minutes. Some of the best stones and crystals include amethyst, black obsidian, and purple fluorite.

Some foods are incredibly helpful at helping people hone their intuitive senses. Each chakra has one or more specific foods that help them remain open and healthy. Some of the specific third-eye chakra foods to make a consistent part of your diet include dark chocolate, omega-3, and basically any purple vegetable or fruit. You may also add purple clothes to your wardrobe and add touches of purple around your home.

As soon as you have successfully opened your third eye, the next big step for you is to start sending telepathic messages. You should have fun and enjoy the experience!

Chapter Eight: Sending Messages to Others

Once you have opened your third-eye chakra, sending telepathic messages becomes more accessible. Before I get to the techniques you will be using to send telepathic messages, I would like to acquaint you with a few things that could hinder your success in the practice of telepathy. The first thing that could make all your efforts futile is a lack of belief. Sure, you have been reading this book about telepathy, but what is your conviction about telepathy's existence or usability? If you do not believe in something, how then can you use its powers? Your belief system is the very foundation of your ability to send messages telepathically. If you do not believe it is possible, then you will not be able to use telepathy. So, the first step is to make sure of your belief. The moment you believe, everything else becomes super easy. Being skeptical closes your mind to the experience you want to have. While prepping yourself to send a message telepathically to another person, believe that the message will reach the person you want.

Belief starts by overcoming your fear of not getting your desire in reality. Many people start telepathy thinking, "Oh, I don't think I have the gift or anything but let me try it and see anyway." They think like this because they have been made to believe that telepathy is a gift that is only available to a select handful of people. Of course, this is false. Telepathy is a natural gift that is possessed by all of humankind. The critical difference is that most people suppressed their childhood gift and can no longer access it due to dormancy. This, precisely, is why I suggest you begin your journey into telepathy by first opening up your psychic senses and start using them once again. So fear is the basis of the lack of belief. To get started, you must let go of your fear of failure. Fear hinders you from believing that you can have what you want. When you really want something to happen in your life, you let go of fear. You must let go of the negative beliefs so that you can enter the highest vibrational state where your chakras are in a state of alignment. The more confident you are in your ability to make it happen, the more you are surrounded by positive energies.

Once you overcome your fear and believe in your ability, there is very little stopping you from sending telepathic messages using any of the techniques discussed below. Before you proceed, remember that telepathy isn't something you master in one day or one night. If anyone tells you otherwise, feel free to tell them you are not ignorant. Depending on how dormant your 6th sense has been, telepathy can take you days or months to achieve. You can increase your chances by practicing a few minutes every day. Telepathy requires a lot of time, patience, and practice. You are good to go if you are willing to devote enough time to practice every day. So, be ready to put in at least 20 to 25 minutes of practice every day. If you need more time than this for practice, you can add more minutes. Your daily practice's duration is subject to changes based on your personal schedule; adjust as needed.

First, you need someone to practice with every day. You are trying to send a message telepathically, so you will need someone to receive that message. The person you practice with should be near you. As a beginner, you shouldn't try to practice over a distance. It is best to be in proximity to the person you are sending a message to. Second, you need to ensure your mind and body are in a state of relaxation before you go ahead. Sending a message is much easier when you and your practice partner are both in a relaxed state. Your receiver has to clear their mind of the roaming thoughts. Ensure you are practicing with someone that shares your belief in what you are trying to do. Otherwise, this other person may make the process unnecessarily complicated. Visualization is a vital part of the process. So, practice a simple visualization exercise every day to improve your ability to visualize. Visualizing is an effective way of defining your thoughts and focusing them on the present. Now, to the real deal:

Technique 1: Meditation for Telepathy

The room you want to use for this practice should be a place of solitude. It could be your usual meditation room or another room you believe can get the job done. The important thing is to ensure that the room you choose is suitable for practice. If you have anyone around, tell them you would like to be undisturbed for at least 30 minutes. Go into the practice room with your partner and lock the door. A locked room is less likely to be open to distractions and disturbances.

- Close your eyes and practice your breathing exercise. Start with your normal breathing until your breathing becomes deeper and softer.

- Pay attention to the vibrations in all parts of your body. Meditation is about feeling your own body. Feel the vibrations in the soles of your feet and work your way up to the top of your head. As you do this, you should feel every part of your body relaxed and ready.

- Once you have relaxed every part of your body, return your attention to your breathing. The more you feel relaxed, the deeper your breathing becomes. At this time, you may start seeing people, things, wildlife, images, etc.,

- Next, bring your attention to your third eye chakra, as instructed in chapter seven. You may feel a tingle, an itch, or even a little pain. Don't fight the sensations. Use the third-eye activation meditation to open your third eye.

- Once you have opened your third eye, visualize the person in the room with you. Picture their third eye in your mind and focus on the third eye. Imagine a purple circle in the place between their brows. This represents their third eye.

- Envision a ball of purple light coming out of your third-eye chakra. Now, guide this ball of light towards the other person's third eye. Direct the light into their chakra and watch as it enters. The purpose of this is to establish a connection with the other person. Without this connection, you cannot send them a message telepathically. If you do the visualization right, you may experience what is known as the "light body" phase, which is when you feel like you are a body of light connecting with another source of light.

- If you successfully established that connection, then you are a step closer to sending them a message. Whatever you want to say to this person, visualize it going in through their third-eye chakra. Feed the message into the opening for as long as needed. Note that a short message is ideal for practice, especially on your first few practices. The shorter the message, the easier it will be fed into their third-eye chakra.

When the person has received the message, you will get it in your guts. The feeling is unmistakable, and it cannot be faked. Once you feel or know that the message is sent, you should stop. It might take you anything from a few seconds to minutes to send the message. After fifteen minutes of trial with no success, you should take a break from practice and try again the next day. Trying again the same day can put a strain on your mind and make you feel mentally exhausted. Practice once every day. After the session, you will feel several vibrations in your body. Surrender yourself to these vibrations and allow yourself to fully experience them.

Remember that the energy you transmit from yourself to the receiver is not a psychic or energy attack or anything of that sort. The light is needed to pass the message. It would in no way harm your own chakra or theirs. The energy may even revitalize your own and their own chakras. So, this technique is not dangerous at all.

Technique 2: Mind-reading Exercise

As you already know, mind-reading is one of the four telepathic activities. To do this exercise, you need a willing partner. Typically, you shouldn't read someone's mind unless they give you permission. You can read someone's mind if you have reasons to believe that they have malicious intentions towards you or any of your loved ones. You can also practice mind-reading by yourself without telling them what you are doing. This is simply to test how good you are becoming at mind-reading. As usual, you need to make sure that your body and mind are both relaxed. Get rid of any tension or strain in your mind and body.

Focus on this person and visualize their third-eye chakra by picturing a purple icon in the area between their eyebrows. Focus on their third-eye chakra. Picture their thoughts swirling around in their mind. Be intentional with your focus. The more you focus, the clearer the thoughts will become to you. If you would like to take it a notch further, you can use your mind to ask them to perform a simple task. The task may be something like getting you a drink or saying a simple word out loud.

If you want them to bring you a drink, visualize them asking if you would like a drink. Then say yes. Picture as this person goes into the kitchen to bring you the drink. Envision them handing you the drink. Most importantly, picture yourself thanking them for the drink. Showing appreciation is essential. Let the visions run through your mind for some minutes and then let go of the thoughts and return to whatever you were doing. The other person may not stand up to get you the drink immediately. Wait until they carry out the mental instruction.

You might not make it happen the first time you try it but remember that the key is consistency and patience. Keep trying until you get it right. Note that this exercise's purpose isn't to change the other person's will; instead, you will work with their will. It is best to choose a task that they would ordinarily perform of their own will. For instance, if they wouldn't normally bring you a drink, don't send them after a drink.

Technique 3: Remote Viewing Exercise

This exercise is used to receive information from another person over a distance. This information can be in the form of words, images, or emotions.

- Sit comfortably in your meditation room. Firmly place both of your feet on the ground with your back in an upright position.

- Take deep breaths and close your eyes gently.

- Breathe in deeply, then visualize yourself touching the third-eye chakra of the person you want to receive information from. Picture yourself lifting a finger to their forehead.

- Picture a silver cord coming out of their third-eye chakra and attaching to your finger as you visualize this.

- Bring the silver cord to your own third-eye chakra.

- Picture the information coming through the silver cord into your own third-eye chakra. The information may take as much as fifteen minutes before it is conveyed to you, so be patient.

- Open your eyes, stretch, and immediately write down whatever is in your mind. You can also draw if it is an image.

You can use this exercise to find out people's expectations about a job or project so that you can do an excellent job for them.

Technique 4: Remote Influencing Exercise

This is a telepathic training exercise to influence another person with your own thoughts, feelings, and needs. You can use remote influencing to establish a great rapport with people that can help you progress in life. The exercise below can strengthen your ability to send your feelings or thoughts and influence people faster.

- Go to your meditation room. Sit in a comfortable position and plant your feet firmly against the floor. Your back should be straight.

- Deeply inhale and exhale about three times before you close your eyes.

- Focus on your forehead and open your third-eye chakra.

- Envision a silver cord coming out of your third-eye chakra. Focus on the person you want to influence and how you want to do it.

- Picture the silver cord going into the third eye of the other person. Let the cord become attached to their forehead. Breathe in and out and visualize the cord entering deeper as you breathe. Breathe three times.

- Imagine your thoughts and feeling passing through the cord to the other person's third-eye chakra. Set your intention on how you want to influence them.

- The information may take fifteen minutes before it gets to the other person.

Pay attention to the person's behavior in the future to see if the influencing worked.

Technique 5: Remote Broadcasting Exercise

This exercise is useful for sending your own thoughts, feelings, needs, and desires to a bunch of people at once. You can use it to attract more customers to your business or improve people's mood around you. You may also use this exercise when doing a project or business presentation or collaborating with investors.

- Close your eyes gently and take deep breaths.

- Focus on your third-eye chakra and visualize the information you want to send out. Form the image or words in your mind.

- Picture bright, white energy coming out of your body. Project the information you want to send into the middle of the white energy. The message should be embedded within the white energy.

- Feel the energy going from you towards your target audience. Visualize your target audience receiving the energy from you. Once they receive the energy, it means that your audience has received your message.

Before you start establishing a telepathic connection with the people around you, you should first focus on yourself. You need to train your mind against the mind-numbing effects that society exposes you to every day. Thankfully, there are techniques to improve your mind to make telepathy more accessible. One technique that I train my mind with is binaural beats and isochronic tones. This involves listening to recordings explicitly engineered for improving the mind for telepathy. You can listen to headphones, preferably in a room without natural or artificial light. You may also use telepathic games to improve your ability.

Never forget that telepathy takes time and patience. So, don't be in a hurry to communicate telepathically. Take your time and practice until you actually get it.

Chapter Nine: Twin Telepathy

It is common knowledge that twins share a special connection beyond what you see in other siblings. Over the years, there have been reports of twin telepathy across the world. This becomes more fascinating when you realize that some of the twins involved were separated at birth. This proves that twin telepathy is not a myth or manmade fiction. Science has yet to find empirical evidence to support the existence of twin telepathy. However, there are anecdotal pieces of evidence that indicate that twin telepathy is indeed real. The concept of twin telepathy borders on how twins, whether they are identical or not, exchange their thoughts and feelings without using spoken or written words. Evidently, this is telepathy as we know it. But twin telepathy is slightly different because usually, twins don't have to train themselves or do anything. The ability just comes to them naturally, especially in times of distress.

If you are a twin, you have likely experienced this connection with your sibling. There have been instances where one twin experience painful sensations just because the other twin, in another location, is experiencing the same thing. Another thing is when one twin knows in their heart that the other twin is in danger. An excellent example of this is the case of the Houghton twins. Back in 2009, the Houghton twins named Leanne and Gemma had a telepathic experience that highlighted the level of connection between them. On a regular day in 2009, Gemma was at their

United Kingdom home with her twin sister. Gemma was going about her daily routine. Suddenly, she experienced a horrible feeling of terror – she felt like her sister was in grave danger. How could this be? After all, they were in the same house together, and her sister was in the bathroom having her bath. What could be wrong? The feeling of dread was intense, and it wouldn't go away. So, she decided to check on her sister in the bathroom. On getting there, she found something that was both shocking and life-changing for her and her sister.

A few minutes before, Leanne had had a seizure in the bathroom, and she was passed out in the bathtub. At first, Gemma thought her sister was merely washing her hair, but she soon realized Leanne was passed out and submerged under the water in the bathtub. Quickly, she pulled her sister out of the bath and performed CPR on her. Gemma saved her twin's life, thanks to the dreadful feeling that washed over her. If she hadn't telepathically felt what was wrong with her sister, she probably would have lost her that day.

Although reputable scientific evidence doesn't exist to prove the authenticity of twin telepathy, many researchers have conducted studies to determine whether the phenomenon is indeed real. One such example is Robert Sommer, Humphry Osmond, and Lucille Pancyr's study in 1981. This study had 35 pairs of twins as participants. The researchers found that at least 12 of the 35 twin pairs had a telepathic connection to each other. They reported experiencing telepathy in "strange" ways. J.B. Rhine also conducted a study on twin telepathy with Sherry and Terry, a pair of identical twins. According to Rhine, Terry and Sherry could exchange test answers in their head. They were also able to tell whenever either of them felt sick or experienced pain. Rhine's research further tested if the twins could exchange complete sentences with each other through telepathy.

Although identical and non-identical twins can both share this telepathic connection, it was found that the connection is stronger in identical twins than fraternal ones. This might be because identical twins are formed from a single egg, which means their genes are completely identical. Fraternal twins, on the other hand, are from different eggs. Considering the case of Gemma and Leanne

Haughton, both of whom are fraternal twins, it is safe to assume that it doesn't really matter whether the twins are identical or not.

The bottom line here is that a telepathic connection does exist between twins. Nearly every pair of twins has a story that points to twin telepathy. Generally, twins share an innate understanding of their emotional state. Since emotions precede behavior, most twins also behave in the same way and perform the same actions. For instance, twins in different locations may purchase the same item simultaneously or pick up their phones to text each other at the same time. They also have a knack for completing each other's sentences. All of these things happen in people who share close emotional bonds, but it appears to be much stronger in twins because of their birth circumstances. After all, most have been together practically from the very first seconds of their lives. Despite the absence of substantial scientific proof, one cannot deny the telepathic connection between twins.

These telepathic experiences between twins result from a deep emotional bond which makes twins extremely sensitive to each other's thoughts, feelings, and needs. The connection provides a deep empathy between twins. This empathy is intense enough to produce specific physical sensations. Spiritually speaking, the telepathic connection between twins is typically referred to as "twin flame telepathy". Because of their twin flame connection, twins may also share vivid dreams.

Let's discuss what twin flame connection is from a spiritual point of view and how it enables telepathy between twins.

Twin Flame Connection

Twin flame connection refers to a bond between two people who share twin flames. Although you might think that the twin flame only exists in twins, this is not so. The twin flames connection can exist between two people who aren't twins. Everyone is composed of energy, but we vibrate at varying frequencies. Typically, the levels at which one vibrates do not change. It defines who we become and, more importantly, who we associate with. Twin flames vibrate on a similar frequency, and this is why people who share twin flames can do things like telepathy. When two souls operate at the same vibrational level, it becomes possible for them to psychically communicate with each other. The twin flame connection exists even before the mirror souls get to know each other. This explains why many twins have this connection despite being separated at birth. Usually, the connection is subconscious. However, you will become aware of its presence when you begin an active spiritual journey.

A twin flame connection typically appears in shared intuition, telepathy, shared dreams, astral projection, and verbal/visual communication.

When twin flames meet for the first time ever, the first connection they will experience is their shared intuition. This sometimes happens when one has just given birth to twins; both twins may try to move towards each other. This is because of their shared intuition. Mirror souls get unexplainable feelings that don't appear to be theirs, yet they very strongly experience the feelings. This shared intuition is what manifested in the case of the Haughton sister. Gemma felt what was wrong with her sister due to their shared intuition.

Example: You live with your twin. Typically, your twin gets home before 6 PM, and you are used to having them home at this time. It is about time that they get home – the time is 5:30 PM. Suddenly, feelings of extreme disappointment and sadness wash over you. You can't explain these feelings, and you wonder why you are feeling that way. You try to shrug it off, but the feelings become more intense. Almost immediately, your twin arrives; from the look on their face, you can tell that they have had an incredibly disappointing day. They settle down to tell you how horribly nightmarish their day was.

In this example, it is evident that the feelings of sadness and disappointment experienced were that of the twin. Yet, you felt it as if it were your own emotions. This illustrates how shared intuition can manifest in twin flames.

Emotions leave an imprint on mirror souls such as twins. Have you ever walked into a room and felt like you could slice through the tensions with a knife? You can tell that a conflict has just taken place in that room when you feel like this. Anger is a powerful emotion that can surprise you when you experience it from another person's perspective.

Example: You are at school having a class you aren't very excited about. Suddenly, you feel a jarring pain in your foot. The pain goes away as quickly as it came. You are surprised, and you have no idea why that just happens. Although the pain only lasted briefly, the memory doesn't leave you. You cannot stop wondering what caused it. About an hour after that, your twin calls you and tells you they have broken their ankle in a minor accident. That pain you felt in your foot was, in fact, the sensations from your twin's injured ankle.

In this example, you are feeling a physical sensation that is not your own. Twin flames can feel the pain, happiness, and excitement of each other. But pain stands out precisely because it is often removed from the current situation.

Shared dreams and astral projection are other ways that twin flames communicate telepathically. This form of telepathy happens when the twins are in different locations. The pull of the connection is so powerful that the souls of twin flames meet in dream states. This often happens in different ways. For instance, twins may have the same kind of dream. Or they may enter a lucid dream state so they can be together in the astral world. They may also astral-project to travel to the astral plane together. The dream state is when you are in your most authentic form. In this state, no limitations are holding you back. This allows you to operate freely. Your soul naturally moves towards the direction where another soul is vibrating on its frequency in the dream state. When twins are separated, their souls remain in a still state. When the physical bodies are asleep and their souls have the freedom to explore, they tend to find each other.

Visual and verbal communications via the mind also happen between twins. This telepathic communication level is typically unlocked when twins have grown together and progressed in their spiritual advancement journey. This kind of communication is different from the ones in the dream state. The more the bond grows stronger between twins, the stronger their telepathic communication becomes.

What are some essential facts to know about twin flame telepathy?

First, telepathy between twins does not require them to have prior skills. The bond is so strong that the connection just happens even when they have no previous telepathy knowledge. This makes it easy for twins to develop their telepathy gifts more rapidly. Remote touching is also possible with twin flames. This is particularly noticeable when the brain is in Theta state. Theta state is achieved when you let go of your ego and defense mechanisms. At this point, your body and mind become relaxed and open to communication – the same feeling you get during meditation or when you are about to drift off to sleep. Twins can telepathically hold hands across distance and even experience other things that involve physical touches.

If you have a twin flame, you should know that you will always be on the same vibrational level. In other words, your consciousness will always be in tune. Your twin flame energy frequency is unique to you and your twin alone, which makes this possible. The more aligned your energy frequency is, the stronger your telepathic connection becomes. In this sense, a great benefit of twin flame telepathy is that it helps you stay in touch with your other half, no matter how vast the distance between you is. You can easily send your twin something as simple as, "I love you" by remaining tuned in with their frequency. So, send love to your twin using the telepathic connection between you.

Telepathic communication between twins isn't always verbal. Sometimes, it comes in the form of memory. For instance, if you are a twin flame, you may suddenly remember a memory that is far from being yours and yet familiar enough. Or you may experience a deja-vu moment. This happens due to the merging of your energies. When the twin flame union happens, and your energies finally merge, you subconsciously take on specific information from your twin just as they take it on from you.

Interestingly, twins are sometimes unable to reach each other telepathically due to a disruption of energy. As all things in the universe are made up of energy, you sometimes absorb negative energy from others. This results in the congestion or blockage of your telepathic channels of communication. Thus, you must perform specific energy-clearing exercises every day to keep unwanted energies from blocking your channel or communication line with others.

If you are a twin and don't recall ever having a telepathic experience or connection with your other half, you may be experiencing energy blockage and disruption. The first thing you can do is work on clearing and healing your energy centers or channels, i.e., your chakras. Even if you do this on your own, you will be able to help your twin in clearing their blocked energy centers. As you already know, telepathy won't work as it should if the energy centers remain blocked. Use the chakra meditation to clear your energy centers and make them as vibrant as they should be.

Conclusively, twin telepathy may be seamless due to the twin flame connection. But don't expect the experience to be as if you were talking through the mobile phone. The experience is a complex one, and each person's story is unique to them. Yet, you mustn't think of every thought or feeling as a telepathic message. Sometimes, you may be picking up on your own subconscious thoughts and desires. You should be able to discern the difference if you don't over-indulge yourself in a fantasy world created by your subconscious mind. Learning to discern your thoughts from your twin's and other people's thoughts will prove incredibly helpful to you in your spiritual journey.

Chapter Ten: Closing the Telepathic Door

The mind is the doorway to telepathy and other psychic gifts. I always liken the mind to a massive house with its doors and windows wide open. Everything goes in and comes out without filter or checks. Every thought, idea, feeling, desire, need, etc., can enter there, occupy the space, and even cause a disturbance. In this case, no one is controlling what goes on in the mind house. Under a condition such as this, the mind has no barrier to shield it from all thoughts, words, suggestions, and ideas. They all come and go as they please. Often, this the case for most people's minds. It is the default state of things. You, on the other hand, shouldn't allow your mind to operate like this. If you don't learn to control what goes in and out of your psychic doorway with the third eye-opening, you will find yourself bombarded by thousands of bits of relevant and irrelevant information every day.

The best way to protect yourself while keeping your psychic senses and third-eye chakra open is to learn how to close the door and window of your mind. Doing this prevents you from being bombarded by harmful, useless, and unnecessary thoughts which can rob your mind of its health and vitality.

Telepathy happens via an exchange of energy. Therefore, every piece of information that you telepathically access takes a light bite from your energy source. Depending on the type and size of information, some take a severe chunk into your energy supply. For this reason, you must train your mind to only receive relevant information or messages. By learning to close your telepathic doorway, you can bar your mind from unnecessary thoughts, ideas, and feelings. You can choose what to receive and what not to receive.

You might think it is impossible to learn to close and open the telepathic door at will, but it is not. With persistence and consistency, you will learn how to willfully open or close your telepathic doorway. Even if you only learn to do this partially, it will make a tremendous difference in your physical, mental, emotional, and spiritual wellbeing. Mental control and mastery are the keys to closing the telepathic door. Once you train and master this, you will no longer be affected by the thoughts, feelings, and moods of everyone you share a space with.

The three most essential tools for training your telepathic door to close and open at your behest are meditation, mindfulness, and concentration. These three things have one thing in common: they help ground you in the moment. They also help improve your concentration skills, enhance your thinking process, and boost inner peace and fulfillment. We have already discussed how you can practice meditation and mindfulness, so there is no need to repeat that information. But I have simple concentration exercises for you to include in your routine.

Concentration Exercise

The point of concentration exercises is to help sharpen the mind and train it to focus better. I'll be discussing at least three concentration exercises that can strengthen your mental power and heighten your ability to focus. Training your mind is similar to training your body. You train your body by going to the gym at least three times a week. When trying to learn something new, you have to put in hours of practice before getting the basics right. This applies to training the mind too. When trying to train your mind to filter information, you need concentration. And if you want to develop your concentration, it requires a lot of practice. Even a 10-minutes practice every day will make a lot of difference in your spiritual and psychical health.

Naturally, your mind will try to resist you when you start training. The mind does not like to be controlled; it wants to be the one in control. The mind does not appreciate discipline, so it will try to stop you from training it. You will have a hard time mastering your mind. Sometimes, you will forget to train; other times, your mind will induce you into a state of levelness. There are different ways your mind will try to stop you from mastering it. But ultimately, the choice is yours. You are the master of your mind. Therefore, it all boils down to what you want to do.

The concentration exercises will help you train your mind and master it to the point where you can willfully close or open the doorway to your mind. This way, you can filter everything that comes in and goes out of your mind. Always practice your concentration exercises in the same place you use for your meditation. You may either sit on a chair or sit cross-legged on the floor. Practice a quick breathing exercise before you start your concentration exercise. You should use at least 10 to 15 minutes for your daily practice. Start with one exercise and keep practicing only that exercise until you have mastered it. Then move on to another exercise. Do this until you have mastered all the concentration exercises. This might take you days, weeks, or months. Do not proceed to the next exercise until you have mastered the first one.

- **Exercise 1**

Choose any book from your library. Open the book and pick a paragraph to count. Now, count the words in the paragraph you choose. After counting, repeat, and count again to ensure you counted accurately. After doing this a few times, choose two paragraphs, and count again. Increase to a full page as the counting becomes easier. The counting should be done with your eyes. Don't point your finger at the page; just count mentally.

- **Exercise 2**

Pick a word or phrase and silently repeat it in your mind for 5 to 10 minutes. When you notice that your concentration is improving, increase the duration to 15 minutes.

- **Exercise 3**

Count mentally from 100 to 1. Skip three numbers each as you count, e.g., 100, 97, 94, 91, etc.,

- **Exercise 4**

Count in your mind from 100 to 1; don't count from one. When you are done, repeat this exercise. Then, you can increase each count by an additional hundred.

- **Exercise 5**

Take an object like a ball. Focus on the ball. Look at it from all sides without forming any word in your mind to describe it. Just watch it with a blank mind. Do not think anything as you watch the object.

The more you practice these exercises, the faster you will progress in training your mind. Let the process be a gradual one. You will start seeing differences in your concentration skills. Eventually, you will be able to concentrate on anything effortlessly. This will help filter psychic messages.

Turning Off Your Psychic Senses

Awakening your psychic senses can be an overwhelming experience. When you start, the experience will be novel and exciting, especially if you are making progress. You will be even more excited the first time you successfully send a telepathic message. But the fact that these things are all happening simultaneously can make the whole process intense. It can cause a strain on your life. So, occasionally, you might need to shut down your psychic senses. Suppose you feel like you are receiving overwhelming information. In that case, it means there is too much energy coursing through your third eye. In this case, you need to learn how to shut down whenever you feel like it.

First, you must train yourself to get out of your third-eye chakra and out of your mind. It is normal to feel like devoting all your time to advance in your psychic and spiritual development, but don't let it become your entire life. You must spend as much time as possible in your human life. There has to be a balance between your physical and spiritual life. Devoting some of your attention to your social matters is a way of diverting the energy from your third-eye chakra. You shouldn't allow all your energy to go to your third eye. Your mind will be in a much better state if you distribute the energy in other areas of your life.

One way to divert energy is to clean up your home and dispose of the clutter everywhere. Doing a little cleaning and organizing here and there will not only help you distribute energy; it will also help you facilitate a calming environment for your mind. A chaotic home or workspace will also result in a chaotic mind. Therefore, if you take care of the chaos in your home or workplace, you are inadvertently taking care of your mind. Decluttering your home stimulates your lower chakra. Pay attention to your finances as another aspect of your life. Take a walk every day.

Ensuring a balance between your psychic senses and portals is an integral part of your life. You must be balanced with your energy centers and your psychic portals. Telepathy isn't a quick fix to solve a nagging problem, so don't see it as such. Practicing telepathy means you have to spend a chunk of your day in the psychic realm. This can distract you from your relationships and everything else, but you shouldn't let it. Spend as much time as possible on your social relationships. Go out with friends. Hang out with your partner. Visit the park. Take your dog for a walk. Do things that help you remain grounded in reality.

Turning Down Your Chakras

In a previous chapter, I talked about how you can open, balance, and align your chakras. As you already know, your chakras are the energy centers of the body. Energy flows to your physical body through the chakras. So, whenever you feel an overflow of energy, the best step is to turn down your chakra. As I said before, chakras can be overactive or underactive depending on the flow of energy. The telepathic doorway cannot be closed if you don't learn to control the flow of energy in your chakras. You can avoid having an energy overload by turning down the chakras to receive as little flow of energy as possible. To temporarily close the door to your telepathy skill, you need to turn down your energy centers. Turning down the chakras will help you increase your personal energy. It can also help you increase your ability to focus. More important, it can help improve your health and wellbeing. When you close the telepathic door to others' thoughts and feelings, this is usually the end result.

Below are three visualization techniques you can use to turn down your chakra:

Radio Dial Method

This is a handy visualization method for decreasing the inflow of energy to your chakras.

- Sit in a meditative pose. Place your palms on laps and close your eyes. Now, visualize your intuition in the form of a radio dial.

- Observe the volume and see how high your intuitive abilities are. Mentally note your current level.

- Once noted, visualize yourself turning down the volume from wherever it is to 1, 2, or 3.

- Once you have successfully turned down your intuitive dial volume, thank the Spirits and wrap it up.

Thermometer Visualization

This is quite a simple and straightforward method.

- Close your eyes and use the breathing exercise to put yourself in a meditative state.

- Once in that state, picture a thermometer in your mind. The thermometer represents your intuitive abilities.

- Imagine the thermometer level decreasing to the lowest level you want. Visualize as it turns down one by one.

Once you get to your desired level, exhale profoundly and arise.

Flower Method

If you love plants, you will find this technique enjoyable and fun.

- Sit comfortably, close your eyes, and do a quick breathing exercise.

- Now, visualize your chakras – specifically the third-eye chakra and the heart chakra. For energy to go to your third-eye chakra, it must first pass through the heart chakra. Most of the sensitive information sent to the body is received through the heart chakra and the third eye.

- Tune in to the heart chakra as you visualize it. Then, imagine a pink flower appearing over your chakras. The flower represents your intuitive abilities.

- If the flower is fully bloomed, that means your intuition is a hundred percent open. A half-bloomed flower means it is half-open. Almost-bloomed means it is 30 percent open, etc.,

- Do this same thing for the third-eye chakra and all the remaining chakras until you feel like yourself again.

When you are done with any of these exercises, be sure to assess your current state of mind and compare it with how you felt before turning down the chakras. Naturally, you should feel calmer, grounded, and safer. If you feel this way, that means the visualization exercise was successful. As long as you anchor your root chakra to the Earth, your chakras will always stay slightly open. This is better than completely shutting off your chakras. If you want to fully open your chakras once again, you only need to reverse any of the abovementioned techniques.

When you turn down your chakras and turn off your psychic senses, you don't completely lose your intuition. It will still be there whenever you need it. The difference is it will be more dormant than it usually is. This will make filtering easier for your mind. With either technique, you can effectively control what gains access to your mind and what doesn't.

Navigating the secrets of telepathy and psychic development is an exciting process. Ensure you enjoy yourself every step of the way. Do not let your practices feel like a task. Let go of whatever doubt, fear, or worry you have in your mind about your abilities. Instead, embrace yourself as you are. More importantly, open your heart to love and light. The third-eye chakra cannot be opened unless the heart is filled with joy and happiness. So do things that make you happy. If you read this book and don't feel like you are ready to start the telepathy journey yet, don't rush yourself. Wait until you are mentally ready for the journey.

Finally, meditate regularly to stay attuned to your higher consciousness. A relaxed mind and body are unlike any other thing in the journey. Take care of your body by improving your diet, exercise, and other things that affect your physical body. Remember that whatever affects your physical body will affect your spiritual body as well. So, taking care of your body should be a compulsory thing instead of a choice. Again, don't limit yourself. Always find ways to advance in your spiritual journey.

Conclusion

Telepathy is inherent in each and every one of us. It is not a unique gift that is reserved for some special set of people. You can be a telepath if you want to. Anybody can become a telepath. But unlocking your telepathic senses doesn't come so quickly, as you have learned from this book. Telepathy practice requires you to be consistent, patient, and, more importantly, diligent. You must be ready to put in the time and effort if you want to see productive results. Awakening your psychic senses and unlocking telepathy can be the foundation for your spiritual awakening process. When you finally get to that stage, you will be surprised by how you have held yourself back from spiritual and physical advancement.

Here's another book by Mari Silva that you might like

Your Free Gift (only available for a limited time)

Thanks for getting this book! If you want to learn more about various spirituality topics, then join Mari Silva's community and get a free guided meditation MP3 for awakening your third eye. This guided meditation mp3 is designed to open and strengthen ones third eye so you can experience a higher state of consciousness. Simply visit the link below the image to get started.

https://spiritualityspot.com/meditation

References

10 Tips To Develop Your Psychic Abilities. (n.d.). PRWeb. Retrieved from https://www.prweb.com/releases/2013/2/prweb10316846.htm

Are Auras Real? 15 FAQs About Color, Meaning, More. (2018, December 3). Healthline. https://www.healthline.com/health/what-is-an-aura

Aura Cleansing: Five Simple Ways You Can Cleanse Your Aura | How to Cleanse Your Aura. (2019, December 17). The Times of India. https://timesofindia.indiatimes.com/life-style/health-fitness/home-remedies/five-simple-ways-you-can-cleanse-your-aura/photostory/72839682.cms

Auras...Colors, Shapes and Sizes. (n.d.). Www.the-Auras-Expert.com. Retrieved from https://www.the-auras-expert.com/auras.html

Babich-Savin, B. (2019, April 17). *Protect Your Aura.* Motivate Your Life-C. https://www.barbarasavin.com/post/protect-your-aura

ChangeYourEnergy.com. (n.d.). *How to Sense Energy for Energy Mastery.* Change Your Energy. Retrieved from https://www.changeyourenergy.com/blog/2311/how-sense-energy-for-energy-mastery

COLORS. (n.d.). Auraology. Retrieved from https://www.auraology.net/colors

CorePower Yoga. (n.d.). Www.Corepoweryoga.com. Retrieved from https://www.corepoweryoga.com/blog/how-clean-your-aura

Energetic Anatomy: A Complete Guide to the Human Energy Fields & Etheric Bodies. (2016, October 11). Conscious Lifestyle Magazine. https://www.consciouslifestylemag.com/human-energy-field-aura

Energy and Spirituality. (2015, June 12). *Energy and Spirituality.* HealingEarth. https://healingearth.ijep.net/energy/energy-and-spirituality

Energy Reading 101: What Your Aura Colors Say About You. (2020, July 19).

Mindbodygreen. https://www.mindbodygreen.com/articles/aura-colors-and-their-meanings

How to Become a Clairvoyant Medium | Subtle Energy. (2020, June 13). Subtle Energy Sciences. https://subtle.energy/how-to-become-clairvoyant

mindbodygreen. (2019, April 23). *mindbodygreen.* Mindbodygreen. https://www.mindbodygreen.com/0-91/The-7-Chakras-for-Beginners.html

Savin, B. E. (2016, October 9). *Protecting Your Energy and Your Aura.* InnerSelf. https://innerself.com/content/living/health/healing-disciplines/13745-protecting-your-energy-and-your-aura.html

Tanaaz. (2016, April 26). *The 7 Layers of Your Aura.* Forever Conscious. https://foreverconscious.com/7-layers-aura

The Seven Aura Layers, Their Functions and Meaning. (n.d.). Www.Violetaura.com. Retrieved from https://www.violetaura.com/resources/articles-library/the-seven-aura-layers

The Seven Layers of the Aura Simply Explained. (2014, July 15). Reiki Coaching Therapy.

Your Pet Has An Aura Too; Here's How You Can Communicate With It | Spirit Science. (n.d.). Retrieved from http://thespiritscience.net/2016/07/14/your-pet-has-an-aura-too-heres-how-you-can-communicate-with-it

Mental Telepathy is Real. (n.d.). Psychology Today. Retrieved from https://www.psychologytoday.com/us/blog/long-fuse-big-bang/201503/mental-telepathy-is-real

(PDF) Telepathy: Evidence and New Physics. (n.d.). ResearchGate. https://www.researchgate.net/publication/323811942_Telepathy_Evidence_and_New_Physics

Telepathy | Encyclopedia.com. (n.d.). Www.Encyclopedia.Com. Retrieved from https://www.encyclopedia.com/medicine/psychology/psychology-and-psychiatry/telepathy

Printed by Libri Plureos GmbH in Hamburg, Germany